FOSTERING RESILIENCY

**CORWIN
PRESS**

The Corwin Press logo—a raven striding across an open book—
represents the happy union of courage and learning. We are a
professional-level publisher of books and journals for K–12 educators, and we are committed to creating and providing resources that
embody these qualities. Corwin's motto is "Success for All Learners."

FOSTERING RESILIENCY

Expecting All Students to Use
Their Minds and Hearts Well

Martin L. Krovetz

CORWIN PRESS, INC.
A Sage Publications Company
Thousand Oaks, California

For information:

Corwin Press, Inc.
A Sage Publications Company
2455 Teller Road
Thousand Oaks, California 91320
E-mail: order@corwinpress.com

SAGE Publications Ltd.
6 Bonhill Street
London EC2A 4PU
United Kingdom

SAGE Publications India Pvt. Ltd.
M-32 Market
Greater Kailash I
New Delhi 110 048 India

Printed in the United States of America

Library of Congress Cataloging-in-Publication Data

Krovetz, Martin L.
    Fostering resiliency: Expecting all students to use their minds
and hearts well / by Martin L. Krovetz.
        p. cm.
    Includes bibliographical references and index.
    ISBN 0-8039-6633-4 (cloth: acid-free paper)
    ISBN 0-8039-6634-2 (pbk.: acid-free paper)
    1. School management and organization—California—Case studies.
    2. Resilience (Personality trait) 3. Educational change—California—
Case studies. I. Title.
LB2805 .K688 1998
371.2'009794—ddc21   98-25457

This book is printed on acid-free paper.

99 00 01 02 03 04 05 7 6 5 4 3 2 1

Corwin Editorial Assistant: Julia Parnell
Production Editor: Wendy Westgate
Typesetter/Designer: Rose Tylak/Lynn Miyata
Cover Designer: Tracy Miller
Indexer: Molly Hall

Contents

Preface   vii

Acknowledgments   xv

About the Author   xvii

1. **What Is This Resiliency Stuff?**   1
   Anzar High School   11

2. **Becoming a Resilient School Community:**
   First Things First   22
   First Things First—The Head   23
   Rosemary School   26

3. **What's In It for Me?**   35
   Cesar Chavez School   47

4. **I Care, You Care, We All Care:**
   But How Do Students Know That?   57
   Moss Landing Middle School   65

5. **Providing High Expectations and Purposeful Support**   73

    Stipe School   86

6. **Valuing Meaningful Student Participation**   93

    Homestead High School   99

7. **Managing Change:** *On Your Mark, Get Set, Are You Ready to Go?*   106

    Mission Hill Junior High School   122

8. **Commonly Asked Questions About Resiliency** *(And the Answers)*   137

Afterword   144

Resource A: Observation Checklist   146

Resource B: Assessing School Resiliency Building   156

Resource C: Moving From Risk to Resiliency in Our Schools   160

Resource D: Cupertino Union School District, Junior High Assessment. Standard 1: Student/School Connectedness   162

Resource E: Questions for Reflection   170

References   176

Index   179

Preface

"How do you like my school?" asked Maria.

"I'm very impressed by how friendly everyone is," said I.

"More important, they really trust me here," said Maria.

Maria is saying a lot about the relationship she has with adults at her school. She is saying that she feels welcome and safe at the school. Of equal importance, she feels valued, respected, and known by the adults at the school.

Few schools successfully foster this kind of relationship with the large majority of their students. After reading this book, I hope you will be motivated to seek out such schools in your community and work to support the deep commitment and hard work that it takes to sustain them. Truly believing in the potential of all students requires changes in daily practices that are deeply embedded in school culture. This book will encourage you to look at your own deeply held beliefs and offer you tools to examine and redesign the school's culture and practices. It will take considerable skill and courage to lead this effort. Be skillful! Be courageous!

Seeking Exemplary Schools

Fostering Resiliency: Expecting All Students to Use Their Minds and Hearts Well is the story of seven schools fighting for the hearts and souls of their students. The adults in these schools know their students and their students' work well. They also know their colleagues and their colleagues' work well. As professionals, they accept the responsibility to work with students, parents, the community, and colleagues to create a learning community in which every student is expected and supported to learn. And they come to school knowing how important their work is.

Initially, Corwin Press asked me to travel and to write about schools that best exemplify fostering resiliency for their students. In March 1997, I visited New York City and observed three extraordinary, small, public high schools serving primarily students of color: Vanguard Academy, Urban Academy, and the acclaimed Central Park East Secondary School (CPESS). I also went to New Hampshire to visit Souhegan High School, a very innovative school serving middle- and upper-middle-class students. Several years earlier, on two separate occasions, I had visited Maria's school, South Pointe Elementary School in Dade County, Florida, a school I had read about because it was being governed jointly by a private company and the Dade County School District. These are wonderful schools from which we can learn a lot.

Why, however, should I or you have to look far from home to find schools that demonstrate a deep commitment to every student? Such schools should and do exist in every community. The leaders of these schools are courageous and need our voices and support. One of these leaders may be you!! Given that school leadership comes from many sources—administrators, teachers, classified staff, parents, students, and community members—reading this book may help you become such a leader.

The seven schools described in this book are located in seven different school districts, a choice I made on purpose to emphasize the presence of such schools in a variety of communities. All seven schools are within 45 minute drives of my house.

Potential of All Students

Fostering Resiliency is much more about the passionate belief in the potential of all students and what it takes to foster that potential than it is about seven particular schools. More than any other single factor, the lack of a deeply held belief in every child's ability leads to students achieving at levels lower than their potential. Most teachers enter the profession believing that every student can be successful, but few experienced teachers hold on to that belief. I do not hold individual teachers or administrators accountable for this. Our society clearly does not believe in the potential of every individual. Our financial priorities as a nation demonstrate our lack of commitment.

At the same time, many of our school practices get in the way. Large schools, large classes, teacher isolation, lack of adequate instructional resources, poorly conceived professional development, inability to stay focused on what is most important . . . these lead to far too many compromises by teachers and administrators, and thereby to a lowering of expectations for students and for themselves. It is not possible for an elementary school teacher, responsible for teaching reading, writing, math, social studies, science, physical education, and music to 33 students, to demonstrate caring for each of the students. It is not possible for a high school or middle school teacher, responsible for 150 to 200 students, to know each student and the student's work well. It is even harder when multiple languages are spoken by the students, or the societal problems of poverty, drugs, racism, and struggling families impose on the lives of the children and adults in our schools. How can teachers in this situation value the participation of each student? In fact, most teachers welcome students being out sick or cutting classes because the number of bodies is reduced. Most teachers demand that students sit quietly and listen to the teacher talk because the teacher is overwhelmed by the demands of the job. And yet, there are schools that are working to remove roadblocks to student success.

Resiliency

My vision for the community I want to live and work in is based on resiliency theory (RT)—the belief in the ability of every person to overcome adversity if important protective factors are present in that person's life. RT is founded on the proposition that if members of one's family, community, and/or school care deeply about you, have high expectations and purposeful support for you, and value your participation, you will maintain a faith in the future and can overcome almost any adversity. When the school community works together to foster resiliency, a large number of students can overcome great adversity and achieve bright futures.

This Is Not a Simple Fix!

As you read about the seven schools featured in this book, you will come to understand the depth of change in school practice and in school culture required to foster resiliency for all students. Fostering resiliency starts by challenging our underlying beliefs about student potential and how students learn. This strikes at the heart of not only who we are as educators but who we are as people.

Thus, fostering resiliency involves far more than altering the discipline policy, adding social service support to the school, adopting a new curriculum program, buying computers, or having teachers go through a new staff development program. As you read this book, you will come to understand that for a school to attempt to foster resiliency for all its students honestly, school practices must be examined. What we teach, how we teach, and how we assess are all central to fostering resiliency. How we organize the school and how we group students are central. Likewise, expecting and supporting all students to be literate and to demonstrate the habits of mind to think critically are directly related to fostering resiliency.

RT serves as a lens to guide school redesign. Look critically at school practices—How does this practice demonstrate caring for every student? How does this practice demonstrate high expectations for every student and support students' efforts to meet these expectations? How does this practice demonstrate valuing student participation?

Focusing my writing on schools is not meant to reduce the important role of family and community.

Organization of the Book

As you read this book, it will be obvious that I have been heavily influenced by the research of Emmy Werner and the writing of Bonnie Benard (1991, 1993, 1995). In 1963, Emmy Werner and Ruth

Smith began to follow the lives of 614 eight-year-olds, all born in 1955 to plantation workers on the island of Kauai in Hawaii. Werner and Smith have followed these people's lives for over 30 years; one of these people tells her story in Chapter 4. Bonnie Benard has taken the research and translated it into a model that has great relevance for schooling and community development. In Chapter 1, "What Is This Resiliency Stuff?" I present the concept of resiliency, summarize Benard's model and Werner and Smith's research, write about gangs as resilient communities, and present Anzar High School—a small, rural, public high school that is demonstrating what can happen when a community believes in the potential of every student. Within Chapter 1 and continuing throughout the book, I include reflective questions. The influence of this book on your practice will be much greater if you take the time to answer these questions as you read. I have included Resource E as space for you to do reflective writing around these questions. I could have placed the questions at the end of each chapter rather than within; however, I feel that your reflections on these questions are important as you read.

In Chapter 2, "Becoming a Resilient School Community," I present a model for moving schools toward becoming more resilient learning communities and present Rosemary School. When I introduced several educators in Campbell Union Elementary School District to Bonnie Benard's writing, they told me to visit Rosemary. They claimed that Rosemary is the kind of school Benard describes, and has been for 30 years. It is!

In Chapter 3, "What's in It for Me?" I discuss the reasons why a school community should want to foster resiliency for its students and staff and what gets in the way. I also present Cesar Chavez School, a school located in one of the poorest neighborhoods in East San Jose, a school with almost no native English-speaking students, a school with an extremely high rate of student mobility, but a school whose staff exudes an infectious and deeply held commitment to each and every student.

In Chapters 4, 5, and 6, I discuss the protective factors—caring, high expectations, participation—at the core of RT. In Chapter 4, "I Care, You Care, We All Care," I present Moss Landing Middle School (MLMS), a school that has redesigned its curriculum, instruction, and student assessment practices to know students and their work well. MLMS is a very caring community of learners. In Chapter 5, "Providing High Expectations and Purposeful Support," I present Stipe School, an elementary school clearly focused on the expectation that every student will be literate at or above grade level and dedicated to the belief that if the school community provides appropriate and purposeful support, based on knowing students and their work well, this will happen. In Chapter 6, "Valuing Meaningful Student Participation," I present Homestead High School, a large comprehensive high school located in a mostly affluent community that has for the most part felt satisfied that the school was doing an excellent job. Homestead has been a leader in Northern California in school restructuring, and many of the school leaders believe in the importance of students participating in their own learning and in the life of the school. In each of these three chapters, I offer a brief list of what I look for when visiting a school to determine if the school culture, curriculum, instruction and assessment practices, and roles of teachers and administrators support the fostering of resiliency. As you read this book, you will come to understand the depth of change in school practice and school culture required to foster resiliency for all students.

The key to school redesign is to improve the quality of life and learning for all members of the school community. Students, teachers, staff, administrators, parents, and district office staff all need to feel cared for, all need to know that expectations are high, all need to know that they are supported, all need to know that their participation is valued.

The primary purpose of this book is to help school leaders understand and apply RT as a guide for proactive, systemic school redesign. The first six chapters should give the reader a sense of how schools that are fostering resiliency look, sound, feel, taste, and smell in practice. Systemic change is not exportable, however. Experience and research clearly tell us that one cannot take what one school is doing, bring it unchanged to another school, and see the concept implemented successfully. The writing of William Bridges (1991) has been a major influence on my thinking. Change is external, and transition is the internal process every person goes through to adjust to the external change. Leading and managing school change is really about caring, high expectations and purposeful support, and valued participation that is carefully planned and orchestrated to help every individual transition. Chapter 7, "Managing Change," discusses how schools and people change and tells the story of Mission Hill Junior High School. Mission Hill has been involved in a major redesign effort since 1991.

You will have many questions about RT and implications for schooling. Over the last 5 years, I have used Bonnie Benard's (1991, 1993, 1995) writing as a starting point in my teaching and work with schools. In the last year, knowing that I was writing this book, I have asked people to write down their questions. In Chapter 8, I present my top 10 list of commonly asked questions about resiliency, along with my answers.

15,000 Hours—Does It Matter Which School a Child Attends?

Children spend approximately 15,000 hours in K-12 schooling. Michael Rutter (1979) asked whether a child's experiences at school have any effect. Does it matter which school the student attends? These questions led Rutter to study 12 inner-city London secondary schools in depth. He used four measures of student outcomes: attendance, pupil behavior, examination success, and delinquency. His research indicates that the school attended does make a difference. He found that schools differ markedly in the behavior and attainment shown by their pupils, and schools that performed better on one of the four student outcomes generally performed better on the others.

Caution: Resilience Is a Relative Term

Few people make it through childhood, adolescence, and adulthood without many ups and downs. Everyone experiences periods of serious suffering. As Weissbourd (1996) writes, "children described as resilient are often simply children who have not yet encountered an environment that triggers their vulnerabilities" (p. 40). Nothing is fixed. Children who are in trouble at one point in their lives often right themselves at some later point. In fact, it is difficult to predict which children in high school will thrive as adults. Often, those selected as most popular or most likely to succeed in high school struggle as adults, whereas others who struggled socially as teenagers appear to adapt very successfully as adults.

A Final Note

It is November 8, 1996. I am sitting in a bakery in Berkeley, California, with Emmy Werner. We have not met before. I am telling her about my ideas for this book. She immediately offers two challenges:

1. "Beware of how you use the term *resiliency*. It is being abused by people seeking grant money. It has been used by both Clinton and Dole in the recent election campaign. The cover story for the November 11, 1996, *U.S. News and World Report* (Shapiro, Friedman, Meyer, & Loftus, 1996) is on resiliency. There is even a brand of panty hose and a face cream called Resilience."

2. "Please, please, please, do not write a testimonial to schools you like. Demonstrate that these schools are affecting student outcomes in positive ways."

The seven schools described in this book are truly caring places, where expectations are high for every student, and adult and student and adult voices are valued. None of the most important work at these schools is based on add-on projects and soft money. In all honesty, and in all seven cases, the work had begun before they ever heard of resiliency, Emmy Werner, or Bonnie Benard.

It is, of course, difficult to demonstrate that schools make lasting differences in people's lives. This book is neither a longitudinal study like Emmy Werner's nor a quantitative study like Michael Rutter's. In response to Emmy's challenge, however, I do include information about student outcomes at the end of each case study that indicates, at least to me and to the school staff, that these schools are having a positive influence on the lives of children.

◆ ❖ ◆

This book is dedicated to
the memory of my parents,
Shirley and Ben Krovetz,
and my grandparents,
Ida and Joe Krovetz

◆ ❖ ◆

Acknowledgments

This book has been largely inspired by the research of Emmy Werner and the writing of Bonnie Benard. Resiliency theory has become the focus of my teaching and work with schools in the community, largely due to how clearly the idea of fostering resiliency speaks to the reasons why I am an educator.

I also wish to acknowledge the writings of Roland Barth, Deb Meier, Ted Sizer, and William Bridges. Much of my own vision for schooling has been formulated thanks to their clarity of reflection.

I want to thank the following people for their input into the lists of what to look for when visiting schools: Gary Bloom, John Erkman, Rose Marie Garcia Fontana, Kathy Gomez, Bill Honig, Lois Jones, Steve Jubb, Michael Kass, Dale Kinsley, Caroll Knipe, David Krovetz, Linda Lambert, Michele Lew, Deborah Meier, Cindy Moore, Steve Myers, Carol Piraino, and Hudi Podolsky. E-mail certainly makes gathering input simple. I was pleased by the number of respondents to my requests for input, and even more pleased by the number of correspondences that resulted among those responding to my requests.

Also, thanks for the input into the top 10 questions in Chapter 8: Susan Campbell, Kathy Gomez, Glen Ishiwata, and Robert Topf.

The graphic in Chapter 2 was designed by Cindy Moore.

As I wrote drafts of each of the seven school descriptions, people associated with the schools gave me feedback.

Anzar: staff—Demian Barnett, Gary Bloom, Marilyn Breiling, Charlene McKowen, Amanda Morgan, and Jean Zlotkin— and students—Kelly Ann Armour, Alex Chavez, Azucena Gomez, Joan Goodspeed, Moshe Kalaani, Gabriel Martinez, Magdalena Rios Metcalf, Melissa Tankersley

Rosemary: Gerry Chartrand, Sue Darchuk, Connie Elness, Charese Fernandes, Jody Latter, Cindy Moore, Sherry Turner

Cesar Chavez: Rosalie Bermudez, Andy Diaz, Ida Larsen, Kathleen LeClaire, Eva Ruth, and Antonio Vela

Moss Landing: Tom Hiltz, Keith Parkhurst, Kathy Rosen, and Barbara Rosenthal

Stipe: Manny Barbera, Lisa Barlesi, Karen Blom, Edwin Dias, Kathy Harris, Alma Maldonado-Cast, and Consuelo Montoya

Homestead: staff—Dorothy Mansfield, David Payne, Lauri Steel— and students—Mike Han, Shine Ling, Molly Odell

Mission Hill: Donna Cohick, Janet Fogel, Laura Hamby, Roy Nelson, Ralph Porras, Diane Smith, and Jackie Tuttle

To Marsha Speck, my colleague and friend and with whom I developed the school change model presented in Chapter 2 and the urban high school leadership preparation program, our work together inspires me.

To my wife Judy, my children Marc, Ted, and Emily, their spouses Zhong Lin, Emma, and Ken, and my grandchildren Hannah and Avery, I hope that I am helping to foster your resiliency. You are at the core of my resilient community.

To longtime friends and family, read about yourselves in Chapter 1. I appreciate the lifetime of fostering resiliency that we have given each other.

About the Author

Martin L. Krovetz is Professor of Educational Leadership and Development at San Jose State University (SJSU). His interests include fostering resiliency, whole school systemic reform, teacher leadership development, and the relationship among the three. He has helped develop two innovative programs at SJSU—a master's program in teacher leadership and an administrator preparation program centered on urban high school issues. He is a former high school math teacher and was a high school principal from 1977 to 1991. From 1988 to 1991, while he was the principal, Soquel High School was 1 of 18 schools chosen nationally to be a member of the Association for Supervision and Curriculum Development (ASCD) National Restructuring Collaborative. He has presented at many national conferences, including ASCD and the Coalition of Essential Schools Fall Forum. He has published widely, including articles in *Kappan* and *Educational Leadership*. He received a BA from the University of Florida and an MA and PhD from the University of North Carolina. He can be reached at One Washington Square, SJSU, San Jose, CA 95192-0072 or via e-mail at MKROVETZ@AOL.COM.

Chapter 1

What Is This Resiliency Stuff?

Can our students really meet our expectations for each of the six exhibitions for graduation?

Well, who are you concerned about?

How about Jill? She is a special education student.

I work with Jill every day. She is doing well in all her classes. She is coachable and motivated. She will be intimidated at first, and she'll need extra help, but if her adviser and I work closely with her, she'll pass all exhibitions.

How about Louisa? Her English language skills are still weak.

We've already agreed that students can do the oral part of the exhibitions in their primary language as long as they do a major part of one in a second language. Louisa can choose to present in Spanish as long as one substantial presentation is in English. We have a rubric in place for second language.

You're right. Louisa will do fine.

How about Jack?

Jack is my advisee. We all know him well. He is lazy and has a
behavior problem, but he is capable. We will work with him
and with his parents. Hopefully he'll choose to take this seriously to graduate. If he does, he'll do fine!

This discussion and ones like it take place regularly at Anzar
High School. Anzar is a small, rural high school, founded on the
principles of the Coalition of Essential Schools. Due to its small size
and its commitment to a strong student advisory program, all students are known well by teachers. I serve as a coach for the Anzar
staff, meeting with them at least weekly. Conversations like this one
occur often and typically involve the entire staff. The conversation
above included comments from six teachers. The case study at the
end of this chapter describes the school in more detail.

Unfortunately, few teaching staffs know their students and student work as well as the Anzar staff does. Few schools are focused
on what is best for students. Within most communities, however,
you should be able to find an Anzar, a Rosemary, a Cesar Chavez, a
Moss Landing, a Stipe, a Homestead, a Mission Hill. After you read
this book, I hope that you—as a teacher, an administrator, a parent,
a community member, a student, a staff member, a grandparent, a
school board member—will seek out such schools in your community and work to support the deep commitment and hard work that
it takes to sustain these schools. Also, I hope you will ask why every
school is not more like these schools and help remove the obstacles
for schools that are striving to be resilient learning communities.

Definitions

Resiliency is "the ability to bounce back successfully despite ex-
posure to severe risks" (Benard, 1993, p. 44).

A *resilient community* is a community focused on the protective
factors that foster resiliency for its members: 1) caring, 2) high
expectations and purposeful support, and 3) ongoing opportunities
for meaningful participation.

Schools in general are terrible at being resilient communities. Most schools and most classes are too large and the school day is too harried for teachers or administrators to know each student well and therefore to care deeply about each student, to set high expectations, to offer purposeful support, and to value the participation of each student.

> **Think back on your own schooling. Who cared deeply about you? Who held high expectations for you and supported you to meet these expectations? Who valued your participation?**

Turn to Resource E and use the space provided to reflect on this question and on subsequent questions. If you do so, even if you take just a few seconds for each question, you will find this book to be much more useful.

Whatever Happened to That Old Gang of Mine?

> **Think back on your own childhood. Who cared deeply about you? Who held high expectations for you and supported you to meet these expectations? Who valued your participation?**

Unlike schools, *gangs* are very resilient communities and they come in all sizes, shapes, and forms. My gang was my group of friends with whom I walked home from school, played ball at the corner playground, and went to synagogue, boy scouts, camp, and 88th Street Beach. They are the friends I played with when our parents socialized together. These friends, my gang, were a very positive force in my life.

My other gang was my extended family. We spent every Sunday at my grandparent's house. So did my aunts, uncles, and cousins. I was the oldest grandchild, and the only male for many years. I received incredible love, attention, and validation. It was also made clear to me that expectations were high—the family carpeting store was named Benmor, not Benmor and Son. My father and mother were clear with me—I was to go to college and do something important with my life. It was also made clear to me, that, as the oldest, I had certain responsibilities to "be a good boy, a mensch" and to lead by example. I was lucky. My gangs provided a positive resilient community for me.

When I finished my PhD, I moved to California, far from family and friends. I married a woman from Iowa, divorced with two young sons. We found that the family gang did not exist for us or for our children; family and old friends were too far away. The gang for our children (we added a daughter to the world in 1973) became little league, softball, swimming, water polo, music, scouts. Needless to say, athletic teams, performing arts, and scouting groups are positive forms of gangs. In fact, these constructive activities and gangs offer similar attractions: a sense of purpose, a hierarchical system of discipline, and a chance to prove loyalty to a group. In all likelihood, when you think positively about your school experiences, you think of relationships that resulted from your involvement in these types of activities.

Whatever Happened to That Old Gang of Theirs?

> Think about times when the protective factors were missing from your life. How did this feel? What did you do to cope? What did you learn about yourself and others from these experiences?

Children have a need for social affiliation and, in most cases, choose peer relationships that are constructive rather than destructive. Richard Weissbourd (1996) writes that children's peer groups tend to become destructive when children lack a basic ingredient of healthy growth: positive sources of recognition, especially meaningful opportunities that extend into relations with adults. Children have to believe that they can create a better life. If they have this belief, they will strive. Without the perception of meaningful opportunities, children have less reason to be afraid of the repercussions of their destructive behavior.

As a high school principal, I always advised new students to be involved in some positive aspect of the school, one in which they could make friends and receive positive adult attention easily. I suggested they become involved in the choir, band, school newspaper, athletics, student council, and the like. Without this positive connection, new students would find that the students on the fringes of the campus were much more open to making new friends than the students who were already involved in positive ways within the school community. For many years, I initiated and facilitated a school service club, one of the primary functions of which was to welcome other students into constructive activities at the school.

Shame is very common among adolescents and children. Weissbourd (1996) reports on research with prison inmates that indicates that many criminals report having been chronically humiliated in their youth.

In my experience, many high school students do not feel valued and do feel shame in the school setting. Often this occurs in one or more of the following three areas:

• Classroom: Many students find classroom learning to be irrelevant to their lives, and whereas many alienated students are behind in their academic skills, primarily reading skills, many are gifted students bored by the lockstep nature of classes. They feel shamed by their teachers for not doing homework, for not performing well, and by their poor grades, and attend less and less regularly.

• Physical education: Although some alienated students are not athletic, many are excellent athletes, often surfers and skateboarders in my community. They dislike the competitive nature of physical education classes and are "shamed" by teachers and peers for not caring about winning. They dislike the special status given to the recognized school jocks. They stop dressing for it and stop attending.

• Peers: In any school, it is clear which groups are "in" and which groups are "out." The in group usually occupies a central place in the school, physically as well as statuswise. Many alienated students feel hatred and shame when in contact with the in group. They will not walk in certain areas of campus, feel lack of ownership and connection to the school, and attend less and less regularly.

For several years while I was the principal of Soquel High School, we offered an after-school opportunity class for 9th and 10th graders who were not attending school regularly. These students were told to not be on campus until 2 p.m. daily and were to attend from 2 to 5. These "nonattendees" came to school every afternoon on time. They talked with the teacher and with me about how, for the first time, they felt connected to the school. The students from whom they felt much disrespect had already left for the day. They attended classes with students like themselves and were connected to an adult who cared about them, had high expectations for them, supported them, and valued them. Little did I know at the time that these were resiliency factors. I viewed the school differently as a result of these conversations.

Moving From Risk to Resiliency

> In every child who is born, under no matter what circumstances, and no matter what parents, the potentiality of the human race is born again.
>
> —Agee & Evans (1960, p. 289)

Practitioners in the social and behavioral sciences often follow a problem-focused hospital model to try to address the needs of at-risk people. A problem focus involves identifying the risk factors—dysfunctional family, disease, illness, maladaption, incompetence, deviance—and seeking resources to develop programs to work with at-risk populations. This approach is reactive, in that programs are designed to help people who are already identified as in trouble. In schools, many alternative programs are designed for these populations. Students who are behind academically may be placed in special education classes or in Title I classes. Truant and behavior problem students are placed in in-house detention centers, opportunity classes, independent study, and continuation schools.

The problem focus model offers little help to educational and community leaders who would prefer a more proactive position, who would prefer to build communities based primarily on protective factors that would reduce the need for special programs for at-risk students because fewer students would be at-risk. A proactive position is based on building capacities, skills, and assets—building resiliency. It emphasizes strengthening the environment, not fixing kids.

What Is This Resiliency Stuff?

> Talk with someone who overcame great adversity. To what or whom does this person attribute his or her success? What did this person do to cope? What did he or she learn about himself or herself and others from these experiences?

Based on longitudinal studies, researchers have found that for every child who comes from an at-risk background who later needs intervention, there is a higher percentage of children who come from the same background who become healthy, competent adults. Werner and Smith's (1992) definitive research that serves as the foundation for resiliency theory (RT) is described in more detail in Figure 1.1.

RT is based on defining the protective factors within the family, school, and community that exist for the successful child or adolescent—the resilient child or adolescent—that are missing from the family, school, and community of the child or adolescent who later receives intervention (Benard, 1991; Speck & Krovetz, 1995). Werner and Smith (1992) write that the resilient child is one "who loves well, works well, plays well, and expects well" (p. 192).

Resilient children usually have four attributes in common (Benard, 1991, 1993, 1995):

- Social competence: Ability to elicit positive responses from others, thus establishing positive relationships with both adults and peers
- Problem-solving skills: Planning that facilitates seeing oneself in control and resourcefulness in seeking help from others
- Autonomy: A sense of one's own identity and an ability to act independently and exert some control over one's environment
- A sense of purpose and future: Goals, educational aspirations, persistence, hopefulness, and a sense of a bright future

Most people have these four attributes to some extent. Whether or not these attributes are strong enough within the individual to

Fostering resiliency isn't just putting stuff into an empty box by the teacher, or elder, or whatever else. It's based on countless interactions between the individual child or adolescent or adult and the opportunities (in their) world and the challenges they face. (Werner, 1996, p. 21)

In 1963, Emmy Werner and Ruth Smith began to follow the lives of 614 eight-year-olds, all born in 1955 on the island of Kauai. For the most part, these children were Japanese, Filipino, and part or full Hawaiians. Their parents came from Southeast Asia to work on the sugar and pineapple plantations of the island. Most were raised by parents who were semi- or unskilled laborers and who had not graduated from high school. The primary goal of this longitudinal study was to assess the long-term consequences of prenatal complications and adverse rearing conditions on the individual's development and adaptation to life. The story of these children is told in Werner and Smith's (1992) *Overcoming the Odds: High Risk Children from Birth to Adulthood*.

As Werner and Smith report, the majority of the children were born without complications. One third encountered four or more risk factors before the age of 2, however. Two out of three of this latter group subsequently developed serious learning and/or behavior problems by age 10 or had a record of delinquencies, mental health problems, or pregnancies by age 18. Nevertheless, one out of three of these high-risk children had developed into competent, confident, and caring young adults by age 18. Quite impressively, by age 32, two thirds of the remaining at-risk group were functioning satisfactorily. Assessment of functioning satisfactorily was based on individuals' own accounts of success and satisfaction with work, family, and social life, state of psychological well-being, and their records within the community. For the follow-up at age 32, data for 505 of the original 614 individuals were secured.

Highlights of relevant findings:

• Forty percent of the resilient group had at least some college, compared with approximately 17% of the total population studied and 13% of the cohort with long-term coping problems.

Figure 1.1 The Definitive Research: Emmy Werner and Ruth Smith's Longitudinal Study

- Most of the resilient children had at least competence in reading skills; Werner and Smith emphasize the importance of this finding for educators, adding that effective reading skills by grade 4 was one of the most potent predictors of successful adult adaptation.
- Most of the resilient males came from households where there were structure and rules and had males who served as role models.
- Most of the resilient females came from households that emphasized risk taking and independence, with reliable support from female caregivers.
- For resilient males and females, their ability to recruit substitute parents was a major feature of how they differed from those found not to be as resilient. These substitute parents unconditionally accepted them as they were.
- Resilient children often were pressed into having to care for younger or older family members. This "required helpfulness" seemed to carry over into their adult lives.
- Resilient children had faith that life would work out and a belief that life made sense; this may or may not be linked with organized religion.
- Resilient children were good at making and keeping a few good friends.
- Resilient children took pleasure in interests and hobbies that allowed them to be part of a cooperative enterprise.
- Resilient adults remember one or two teachers who made a difference for them.
- Nowhere were the differences between the resilient individuals and their peers more apparent than in the goals they had set for themselves. Career and job success was the highest priority on the agenda of the resilient men and women, but the lowest priority for their peers with problems in adolescence.

A more recent follow up at age 40 confirms these findings.

Excerpts from "The Faces of Resiliency" by Mervlyn Kitashima, one of the participants in Emmy Werner and Ruth Smith's study, is included as Figure 4.1.

Figure 1.1 Continued

help that person bounce back from adversity is dependent on having certain protective factors in one's life. The following are key *protective factors* needed within the family, school, and community:

- A caring environment: At least one adult who knows the child well and cares deeply about the well-being of that child (see Chapter 4)
- Positive expectations: High, clearly articulated expectations for each child and the purposeful support necessary to meet these expectations (see Chapter 5)
- Participation: Meaningful involvement and responsibility (see Chapter 6)

Where Do We Go From Here?

Think about three students whom you know well, who are different from each other. What does their school do to foster resiliency for each of these students? Specifically, what do people at their school do to help each of them feel cared for, know that expectations are high and support is strong, and know that their participation in the life of the school and classroom is valued? What do each of these students need to experience a more resilient learning community at their school? Use these students as a lens as you continue reading this book and as you look at your school.

Fostering resiliency in children is a long-term project, involving systemic change within the communities of children. It isn't something we do to kids. It isn't a curriculum we teach to kids. It isn't something added to a school or community with short-term grant money.

Supporting resiliency in children is based on deeply held beliefs that what we do every day around children makes a difference in their lives. It is about dedicating our hearts and minds to creating communities rich in caring, high expectations, purposeful support, and opportunities for meaningful participation. It is the understanding that the culture and daily practices of schools need to be redesigned in ways that demonstrate a deep commitment to the potential of all students, and it is the courage to work to create such schools.

As our social institutions have fallen apart—there is no need to outline here the effects of divorce, mobility, long work hours, poverty, racism, sexism, and the like on our children and on society—more and more is expected of schools to meet the social and psychological needs of students. At the same time, schools are being constantly criticized for not preparing graduates with the academic skills to be productive members of the American workforce. In response to a multitude of conflicting demands, many schools lack clarity of focus, offering a program that resembles a shopping mall—lots of independent shops, browsing is encouraged, and buying is optional (Powell, Farrar, & Cohen, 1985).

Yet, there are schools, the rare schools that exist in each of our communities, that maintain high academic standards and at the same time serve as resilient communities for children and adults. The schools presented in this book are fighting for the hearts and souls of their students. They are places where students feel trusted, accepted, supported, and respected. They are places where students and their work are known well by the adults.

Anzar High School

Merrill Vargo, director of the Bay Area School Reform Collaborative (Hewlett-Annenberg school reform initiative), has said to me on several occasions that one of her fondest hopes for school reform is that there will be at least one high school in Northern California that people view as an exemplary model, rather than people going to New York to visit Central Park East Secondary School. Anzar will be that high school.

A School Snapshot

At a staff meeting during spring 1997, we made a list of students who might be in need of additional support. We listed 60 students who fell into one or more of the following categories: special education, English learning, migrant, attendance, behavior, grades. We eliminated approximately 20 names quickly because they were doing well in school. An individual plan was set and implemented for each of the other students. Many had or would have a community mentor to help them with their school studies, to support them in preparing for their graduation exhibitions, or to offer them a career apprenticeship. I know of no other high school where this quality of student focus occurs. When students are known well, they do not fall through the cracks. Some students may not be as academically successful as we would like, but every student is treated respectfully, and no student is written off or forgotten.

Background Information

Anzar High School is a new, small, rural high school located in San Juan Bautista, a mission town south of Silicon Valley. All students work closely with a teacher-adviser throughout their 4-year high school career. The relationship that develops allows Anzar to implement two important programs—service learning and graduation by exhibition. The school is teacher led; there are no administrators or guidance counselors. Anzar is a member of the Coalition of Essential Schools.

My involvement with the Aromas/San Juan Unified School District began in 1991. The Aromas/San Juan Unified School District arose from a grassroots, unification effort initiated by parents seeking student-centered, community-oriented schooling for their children. As part of a unification vote in 1990, a school board was elected to oversee the formation of a new school district and to develop a high school for the two communities to be serviced. Previously, Aromas School was part of a large K-12 school district, which has its own comprehensive high schools. San Juan was a single K-8 school that fed into a neighboring, large comprehensive high school. One of the new board members enrolled in the Educational Administration Program at San Jose State University and was a student in the first class I taught there. We quickly recognized the common vision we had for schools, and I was hired to facilitate the search for the new superintendent. I have stayed involved with the district as a critical friend for the new superintendent, both K-8 schools, and Anzar High School. Three of the initial four high school teachers were teachers I had worked with while principal of Soquel High School, approximately 40 miles away.

High school classes began in the fall of 1994 with approximately 60 ninth-grade students. An additional 40 students joined Anzar High School in 1995, another 50 in 1996, and another 120 in 1997. It is expected that the school will grow to approximately 450 students, grades 9-12, by 2000. These students represent a multicultural population (40% Hispanic; 50% White, not Hispanic; 10% other). The clientele includes special education, fluent-English proficient, limited-English proficient, non-English proficient, Title I, and gifted students.

For its first 3 years, Anzar met in temporary buildings on the Gavilan Community College campus. The new high school facility did not open until fall 1997. During this time, many of the students took college classes for credit. Students continue to do so, particularly for advanced placement coursework. Gavilan is approximately 5 miles from the new campus.

Uniqueness of the School

We know everyone. We know teachers inside out. They are on a first-name basis with you. It isn't by second semester that they are getting to know you; it happens by the second day, or third day max.

—Anzar Senior

Anzar is a special place for students and adults. The smallness of the school and the commitment to a student advisory program mean that every student is known well by several adults. The conversation at the beginning of this chapter is a regular form of conversation at Anzar. I have never been in a school that so consistently makes decisions and has discussions in which the appropriateness of action is so centered on what is best for individual students. Parent and student voices are important in decision making also. In fact, and unique to this school district, one high school student is elected at Anzar to be a voting member of the school board; on several occasions, the student's vote has been the deciding vote on important issues.

In talking with several teachers about how to present Anzar best, we agreed that I should present four important components of the school. We feel that these components demonstrate the uniqueness of the school and are at the core of how Anzar provides the protective factors that foster resiliency for its students.

The Givens

Being new, the culture of the school is being defined every day. Staff, students, and parents have taken the time to agree on the *givens* for the school, however (see Figure 1.2). These are the principles that the school is based on and no longer up for grabs. They guide practice when tough decisions need to be made. When new teachers are hired, we expect that they will come to Anzar because they want to work at a school based on these principles. Teachers may not always be sure how to challenge students to use their minds well, develop exhibitions, design curriculum where depth of coverage is stressed over breadth, coach rather than tell, integrate curriculum, and so on, but they chose Anzar and Anzar chose them because of their desire to be a part of this special school. The teaching staff is truly outstanding!

Yet, school life is never easy. One of the givens is the commitment to full inclusion and to heterogeneous grouping of students. Given the wide breadth of student academic background, teachers struggle every day with meeting the needs of students. They talk regularly about modifying curriculum for special education students and about expectations for English-learning students. They talk regularly about how to motivate and support students who cannot or will not read, and, at the same time, how to challenge motivated students. Several teachers talk about feeling overwhelmed by the demands of differentiating instruction for so many of their students. More students fail classes than we would like. It is hard to find enough time to collaborate on these issues. Teachers often wonder aloud, "Can I handle it here?" "Is it worth it?"

Graduation by Exhibition

To graduate from Anzar, all students must prepare and present six exhibitions—math, language arts, science, social science, service learning, and postgraduate plan. These exhibitions are in addition to more traditional course requirements. The rubric for the exhibitions is based on the *habits of mind* we expect all our students to develop. We call our habits EPERRs (evidence, perspective, extension, relevance, reflection; see Figure 1.3). Students often wonder aloud, "Can

1. **Community**
   Service learning
   Responsiveness to the community
   Community and student input

2. **Inclusion**
   No tracking
   All children can learn

3. **Professionalism**
   Site-based management
   Teachers as administrators
   Teachers planning and teaching together
   Communications guidelines
   Collegiality
   Teachers as learners

4. **Quality**
   Integrated curriculum
   Small class size
   Depth over breadth
   Advisory

5. **(High) Expectations**
   Graduation exhibitions
   Lifelong learners
   Ability to use EPERRs

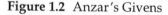

Figure 1.2 Anzar's Givens

I handle it here?" Student comments below indicate that, although "stressed to the max," students recognize the value of the Anzar experience.

These exhibitions are intended to be centered on issues and questions of importance to students that are complex enough for them to explore from multiple perspectives. Students are encouraged to use an interdisciplinary approach and therefore to combine more than one exhibition at a time. All exhibitions have an oral and a written component. Because we value the arts and require some second language proficiency for all students, students are required

Evidence: What do I know and how do I know it?
    What are all the choices?
    Show the evidence.

Perspective: What are the biases—mine and others?
    What do I already know from my past experiences,
        and what's my bias?
    What is the bias of the research used?
    What are alternative points of view?
    What did I learn from the experiences of others?
    Walk in somebody else's shoes.

Extension: What are the deeper implications?
    How might this affect the future?
    What if something changed?
    Is there a pattern here?
    How does this connect to other ideas/issues?
    Go beyond what you know.

Relevance: What difference does this make?
    Why is this important to me?
    How can I use this?
    How does this issue influence the community?
    How is this important to my community?
    What can people do with this information?

Reflection: What did I learn?
    What other questions does this bring up?
    Has what I've done changed my way of thinking?

Figure 1.3 Habits of Mind—Anzar's EPERRs

to integrate both of these into at least one of their exhibitions. Exhibitions are judged by community members who volunteer their time for this purpose. Students know the value of this work. "At first, one of the hard parts is to take a general subject like math or science and put it into a real-life situation, where, if you were just studying out of a textbook, you wouldn't know the difference."

I have judged exhibitions ranging from capital punishment, to the relationship of favorite music to how students dress, to why the guitar is the most influential instrument of the 20th century, to why science fiction literature is more than entertainment, to setting up an after-school sports program for one of the local K-8 schools as a service learning project. I observed exhibitions almost totally in English by two bilingual Latinas, one presented on bilingual education and the other on why Mexicans are not welcome in California. I have judged a math exhibition done by a Latino student who had been in the United States for only 2 ½ years, done totally in English, about the influence of population growth in China; he was able to answer my questions about linear and multiple regression. I have judged an exhibition titled "Is Tree Farming Sustainable in the Future?" that counted for language arts, social studies, math, and science.

One of the wonderful benefits of exhibitions is that a student receives very specific and primarily positive feedback, recognition, and praise from the judging panel, as well as constructive criticism as to how the exhibition could have been stronger. One student said to me, "You get a real sense of accomplishment when you do the first one. You read about exhibitions, and think it's impossible, but when you do it and pass it, it's like I did it and didn't think I could."

Students compare their high school experience to those of friends at other high schools and say, "Our school has a very high bar for achievement that requires that you be on top of things. There is no way to get out of things. There is no way to skate through the system." One of the main complaints I hear from students is that they do not have a laid-back senior year.

Be clear—exhibitions are very different from a senior project. Senior projects usually are a research project done in a special class taken during one semester of the senior year; school practices need not be affected. Exhibitions and EPERRs are the guiding principles for instructional and student assessment practices throughout the school. All teachers are expected to develop curriculum and to use instructional and student assessment practices that prepare students for their exhibitions. Every class is affected.

Of course, a commitment of this magnitude affects the work life of the teachers. A few teachers are given the class assignment of coaching students for their exhibitions. When the coach is an English teacher, however, the student and coach spend considerable time with the math teacher, for example, working on the math exhibition. The time involved is considerable and a necessity if the student is to be supported to do quality work. In addition, the time to coordinate exhibitions—recruiting judges, training judges, copying student written work for the judges, coaching, setting up the rooms, buying refreshments, entering exhibition results on transcripts, maintaining a written and video library of all exhibitions—takes time outside of the regular expectations for teaching. Teachers wonder aloud, "Can I handle it here?" "Is it worth it?"

The School Is Teacher Led

The school employs no administrator. Currently, three teachers are elected each year and given release time to serve as the leadership team. No one may serve for more than 2 consecutive years, and leaders must teach for at least 60% of the day. The school has hired a classified office manager to oversee many of the management functions of the school. Most schoolwide decisions are made in a weekly staff meeting by consensus. As a result, teachers feel full ownership and responsibility for decisions made. Many parents and students also feel ownership due to their involvement on school committees, and, for students, based on schoolwide discussions held in advisories (see Barnett, McKowen, & Bloom, 1998).

Students have spoken with me about the advantages of a teacher-led school. They feel that this encourages teachers to act as a whole. There was no one authority figure "ruling over" the students, and, because of the responsibility all teachers have for the success of students and the school, teachers know students better and value student input.

Advisers are the primary contact with and for parents regarding any and all issues affecting students, including school progress, discipline, and postschool planning. Currently, adviser responsibilities come on top of teaching five classes. We have been unable to figure out a practical way to make advisory part of the regular assignment and still maintain reasonable class sizes. Again, teachers regularly wonder, "Can I handle it here?" "Is it worth it?"

The governance structure also affects parents—they are not always sure who to go to for answers to their questions, and they are used to being able to go to the principal when they want an issue addressed. The role of the superintendent is also different. He is the primary evaluator of all Anzar staff. Unique to Anzar, the teacher leadership team, with union approval, participates in the evaluation of all probationary teachers. The superintendent also sits in on many leadership team and staff meetings and knows the school much better than is true in most school districts.

Time for Planning Is Built Into
the School Calendar

Being part of Anzar can be a burn-out job, and we grapple constantly with how to support the resiliency of the adults. We know that time is the most precious resource to support teacher and school renewal, and we have built in time in several ways for this reason.

Students leave campus an hour and a half early every Wednesday. Staff meetings take place during this time and almost always end at 3:30 p.m. In addition, the David and Lucille Packard Foundation and the Walter S. Johnson Foundation have provided money for 20 paid planning days, used primarily in the summer, for all staff to collaborate on refining the exhibition process, curriculum development, and other issues of importance to the school. These days are in addition to the eight professional development days provided by the state and approved by the school district. There is never enough time, but at least the staff know that, as professionals, they have weekly and summer time to be reflective and collaborative.

Another School Snapshot:
The Students' Point of View

I am sitting with eight seniors. I have told them about my book and have asked them to talk about how Anzar has fulfilled their expectations or not done so. This is Anzar's first senior class. These eight, along with about 35 of their friends, have been the oldest students in the school for their entire high school careers—as they say to me, "We have been seniors for 4 years."

They speak warmly about the high expectations and support they receive from teachers. They each have stories to tell. One of the students left Anzar for her sophomore year to go to a large high school and returned. She talks about how, at the large high school, teachers and counselors did not know her, yet told her what to do. At Anzar, "Teachers take the time to know me well, to give me choices, and to support the choices I make." She also speaks about how at the larger high school, which was 90% Latino, she felt that discrimination occurred toward Latinos in terms of school expectations and among Latino students themselves. At Anzar, she says, each student is seen as an individual and all students get along. She sums up her thoughts: "At the large high school, teachers are committed to their jobs. At Anzar they are committed to students."

The students speak at length about how the graduation exhibitions set a high bar that all students are expected to meet. It is February and only one of the eight has finished all six exhibitions; she is the only student in the school to have finished. They talk about feeling cheated because they are not able to coast during their last semester as their friends at other high schools are doing, and of the stress related to making post-high school plans, finishing required coursework, and preparing exhibitions. They speak of how exhibitions teach them to set goals and meet them; to research, write, speak, and coordinate information; to see how school content relates to real life; to research things other than what teachers teach; to use the Internet, to interview experts, to use several libraries; to work independently, with the teacher as a guide. They talk about the pride and sense of accomplishment they feel as they present their exhibitions, and of their responsibility to be role models to help younger students appreciate the value of the exhibitions and the commitment it takes to do them well.

They also talk about how the smallness of the school brings students together—no cliques, no in groups or out groups; they are all friends. They feel relatively safe from violence, gangs, and drugs. One student says, "The change from junior high school to high school was easy because there were no big classes, and we didn't get drowned out by the other voices." They also speak about missing some of the school activities that exist at the larger high schools—more sports teams and pep rallies. And they speak about missing Gavilan College, where they had had more freedom of movement, better food services, the library, and full science and art labs.

They talk with me about the advantages of a teacher-led school. One student says, "I think the standards are higher here because teachers care about us more. Our relationships are so close that they want the best for us."

Anzar is a resilient learning community. The words of students clearly demonstrate that the students know that teachers care about them, know that expectations are high and that teachers support them, and that their participation in their learning and in the daily life of the school are valued.

In the following chapters, I end each case study with a section on student outcomes. Given the newness of Anzar, I felt that the voices of students, summarized here, should be the student outcomes. Readers are encouraged to visit the school and to serve as judges for student exhibitions.

Anzar High School
2000 San Juan Highway
San Juan Bautista, CA 95045
408-623-7660

Chapter 2

Becoming a Resilient School Community

First Things First

It is 7:20 a.m. I am 10 minutes early for my second visit to Rosemary School. I see a teacher walking across campus toward the main office. I realize that I know him. His ex-wife and my wife work together teaching English-learning students at a high school in a nearby district.

A car pulls into the parking lot. Two young Asian students get out. The teacher yells a hello to both of them by name and to the father. In most schools, the students, and perhaps the father, would be scolded for bringing the students to school 40 minutes early. Not at Rosemary. The two students have big smiles on their faces, as does the father. From the three big smiles, I assume that their days are off to a very positive start.

I was visiting Rosemary School because I respect several educational leaders in the Campbell Union School District, and, after they read Bonnie Benard's (1991) article, they told me that Rosemary is a resilient learning community and has been for 30 years. This seemed an exaggerated claim, given how difficult it is to maintain a positive school culture over time, particularly when the school clientele has changed in recent years as it has at Rosemary. The case study at the end of this chapter is about Rosemary School.

Introduction

If school professionals do not believe deeply that all students can learn to use their minds and hearts well, little else matters. No professional development program, no new instructional materials, and no infusion of technology will make a lasting effect on student learning if the key adults in the student's life do not believe in the potential of each and every student.

> **Do you believe that all students are capable of doing intellectually challenging work?**

When I ask experienced teachers if they believe that all their students can succeed academically, most are unsure or answer in the negative. When I ask these same teachers to remember their first years as teachers, they all clearly remember coming to work with the firm belief that what they did was important, based on the conviction that every one of their students could be increasingly successful in school. Why is it that many teachers lose the sense that what they do every day is important? What can be done so that teachers maintain their sense of purpose?

My colleague Marsha Speck and I have developed a model (Figure 2.1) that presents what we think are the prerequisites that must come into place to support a school creating the conditions to support student success. The components of our model are evolving processes that may have a clear beginning, but have no ending.

First Things First—The Head

> **Think about the three students you reflected on in Chapter 1. Do you believe that each is capable of intellectually challenging work? What evidence do you have? What do you do to challenge each of these students, and how do you support their work?**

Any effort to improve the quality of life and learning for students must begin with an examination of underlying beliefs. This requires a much deeper look than the usual efforts to write a school

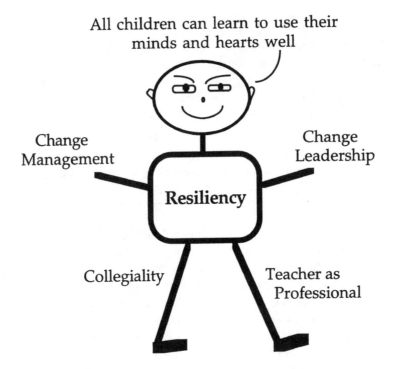

Figure 2.1. Resiliency
SOURCE: Cynthia Moore.

vision statement, by consensus, across various segments of the school community. School leaders need to examine carefully their own underlying beliefs about why they come to work every day and what they believe about students as learners, and then cause their colleagues to undertake the same careful examination.

Implicit in this reflection is the collection of data, especially student work, that is examined to learn if student work offers evidence that the beliefs one professes are in fact occurring in practice.

People have asked me what I mean by "using one's mind and heart well." Go back to the habits of mind (EPPERs) in Figure 1.3. When students demonstrate that these habits of mind are an integral part of how they think and act, they are demonstrating their ability to use their minds and hearts well.

If school staff say that they believe that all students can use their minds well, then if I visit that school, I should see the following evidence:

- Lots of student writing based on students thinking about issues that are relevant and important to students
- Teachers using questioning strategies that require students to think more deeply
- Students at work in classrooms, rather than students listening to teachers working
- Student assessment strategies that evaluate the student's depth of thinking
- Teachers modeling critical thinking through their engagement in action research projects designed to improve their own practice

If school staff say they believe that all students can learn to use their hearts well, then if I visit that school, I should see the following evidence:

- Students working cooperatively in groups in which every student is participating and individual accountability is clear
- Students serving as and receiving peer and cross-age tutoring
- Students engaged in service learning activities
- Students engaged in learning about and contributing to the solution of real issues of concern to the students and to the community
- Teachers modeling by working together as peer coaches and reviewing student work together
- Principals modeling by engaging teachers, students, and parents in meaningful work on school, district, and community issues
- Recognition programs that reward cooperative achievements rather than individual achievements

Please note the depth of change in school practice and school culture that is required. Fostering resiliency is at the core of schooling.

The Right Leg: Collegiality

Schools will not be successful if teacher practice is primarily based on working in isolation from other adults. Teachers need to know each other and each other's work well. Outstanding schools are not composed of 1,000 individual points of light, but instead have a clear beam of powerful, focused light starting from 1,000 sources. Collegiality is discussed in more depth in Chapter 3.

The Left Leg: Professionalism

The redesign of our schools, more than anything else, is a quality of life issue. Teachers and principals need to believe that they are more than "just teachers" or "just school principals." Teachers and principals need to be seen and recognized as professionals; they need to see themselves and recognize themselves as professionals. They need to believe that what happens inside their classrooms, each and every class period, each and every day, is of critical importance, and just as important is what happens outside of their rooms—in other classrooms and throughout the school—and they need to believe that they can influence what happens inside and outside their rooms. Issues of professionalism are discussed in Chapter 3 as related to intellectual stimulation, respect, voice, and job satisfaction.

The Arms: Managing and Leading Change

Being part of a school that truly assesses its underlying beliefs, practices collegiality, respects employees as professionals, and truly is working to be a resilient learning community is courageous work. School leaders need to have the skills, knowledge, attitudes, and behaviors to lead this effort. Chapter 7 focuses on change.

The Heart: Resiliency

Keep reading!!

Rosemary School

An Essential Conversation

What follows are parts of a conversation I had with Harriet Siegel, a retired teacher who taught at Rosemary School for 22 years (1966-1988) and was the school's reading specialist for most of that time. We were meeting for the first time and were sitting in a coffee shop in Campbell. I told her about my book, about how I had heard wonderful things about Rosemary School and had visited a few times. I turned on my tape recorder and asked her to talk with me about why Rosemary is such a special school. The conversation, mostly Harriet talking to me, lasted for about an hour. Pay special attention to her comments that relate to caring, high expectations and purposeful support, and valuing participation.

HS: We looked for teachers who really cared about kids and knew curriculum second. That was our really big thing. The kids came first, and we tried to match the curriculum to the children, not the children to the curriculum.

Our school was in transition. The community was becoming very transient. One September there were 75 new kids coming in, and I met with the teachers. We decided to try four different approaches to reading. Each classroom was set up with appropriate materials. Each kid was tested and placed in a classroom that seemed appropriate for his mode of learning. It was a lot of work. The teachers had an openness to change. They were concerned about kids, and they were concerned about trying new things, and it worked!

I remember when the first Vietnamese students moved into Rosemary. We called parents and said we needed help. They brought us a professor of communication from the University of Saigon. We hired him as an aide. He is now head of bilingual education in a neighboring district. There were a variety of types of classrooms. We placed children where they would be comfortable. Teachers were very, very open. A kid might be in first grade for reading, third grade for math, own grade for social studies. We placed kids where their needs would be met. We were the first school in the state to have a program for Vietnamese students.

Being out of the classroom as a Miller Unruh teacher, I became involved in many professional activities. I became aware of all these nationally known people coming into the area. And what I did, I offered them $100 to come to Rosemary. And the teachers were very open to trying new things.

We were the only school, we were way ahead of the district; they never heard of staff development. They didn't know what it was. There was a core of teachers across grades. We worked together a lot. The principal was new, in his first principalship. He said he knew nothing about reading and turned the reading program over to me and to the teachers.

We fought with the district over retention. We wanted kids not judged by a policy. We always fought for an individual basis. That whole framework of what's best for the kid permeated everything.

Teachers were never punitive. They were always open to looking at why the kids did what they did.

We always took turkeys out to families at Thanksgiving time; teachers still do that. So much caring there.

MK: Where did this tremendous caring come from?

HS: From George, my first principal at Rosemary, and from Monroe, the psychologist. But, we didn't have a lot of good principals.

Caring, the inservice, and the willingness of the teachers to try new things. Nothing was imposed on us. When we would see something new, we would talk about it. We would say, "What do you think? Should we try it? What kind of materials do we need?" That openness to trying new things benefited the kids. Teaching was never dull.

MK: The teachers had to feel safe in this school and district.

HS: Teachers were not afraid. It was really New York chutzpah.

We brought in good staff. No deadheads. You worked your head off, Saturdays and Sundays.

MK: Only a few teachers are left from the old days?

HS: Only three, one of whom is retiring this June.

MK: Yet, the school is continuing on with deep caring about kids. Who has been passing this down from teacher to teacher?

HS: I know what we used to say. When people came to Rosemary, they became absorbed in the Rosemary culture. When teachers come, they don't do their thing, they do Rosemary's thing.

MK: So, as each group has come along. . . Do you know how unusual that is? This has been going on for 30 years.

HS: Well, you know it was a joy teaching at Rosemary. It was a joyful experience.

MK: Because?

HS: Because of the kids. The kids loved coming to Rosemary, but they really came away with something. I remember feeling that people were crazy if they sent kids out to be happy and unable to read. I think the others felt the same. If you are allowed to be part of a supportive group, the creativity juices just flow. And, if your focus is on kids, you just have it.

MK: How much do you think this has to do with Rosemary being the most diverse of Campbell's schools, and teachers feeling they are at Rosemary by choice?

HS: I think that this is an important part of it. There is a feeling of being needed and rewarded. Everything was hug time. I never enjoyed teaching anywhere as much as at Rosemary.

Background Information

Rosemary School is the most culturally diverse of the eight elementary schools within the Campbell Union School District. The school consists of 530 students—49% Hispanic; 27% White, not Hispanic; 12% Asian; 11% African American; 1% other. Ninety-five percent of the students receive free or reduced price lunches. Fifty-nine percent of the students are English language learners, speaking 21 different languages. Many years ago, the school was primarily White, but lower-middle class as compared to the middle-class students in the rest of the district. Later, the population shifted, and the school became predominantly Asian, Vietnamese in particular. In recent years, the population has shifted again and is primarily Hispanic.

During the 1996-97 school year, Rosemary was totally rebuilt on the same piece of land that has housed Rosemary since 1952. The new $9.5 million building was designed to a great extent by the faculty and classified staff. Art in architecture was a major emphasis during the construction. The banners in the lobby, the fence panels, the upstairs screens feature Rosemary children at play. The mobiles in the new exploratorium were created by Rosemary students, then enlarged and sculpted by Campbell Middle School students. State-of-the-art technology is part of every classroom.

Rosemary School has been identified as a Leadership School in literacy by the Noyce Foundation, is a California Distinguished School, received a state grant for school restructuring (SB 1274), and has a Title VII grant for bilingual and dual immersion education.

Uniqueness of the School

First Things First—The Head

It should be clear from Harriet's words that the staff at Rosemary School believe deeply in the potential of each student. My observations have only confirmed that this belief is at the core of what each staff member brings to Rosemary daily. One day, I was talking with seven teachers about Rosemary. I said that I never heard negative talk about students. One teacher responded, "Negative talk is not the Rosemary way." A second teacher said, "We would laugh a teacher out of the school for talking negatively about students." The other teachers laughed and agreed.

When I walk through classrooms, I observe all the characteristics that demonstrate a belief in students' abilities to use their minds and hearts well. Student writing is hanging on walls and from the ceilings in classrooms; teachers are using appropriate questioning strategies; running records and other appropriate assessment strategies are being used to guide practice; interactive writing centers, writers workshops, literacy circles, and other excellent literacy strategies are evident in every classroom; students are active learners; students are working in cooperative groups; peer and cross-age tutoring is occurring.

Hiring the right people is critical. As Harriet stated, teachers new to Rosemary are expected to care about kids and to work long hours. Given the implications of class size reduction in grades K-3 and retirements, there has been a large turnover of staff. In 1997, of the 23 teachers, 8 were in their first or second year. District and school support for beginning teachers is strong. Experience demonstrates that in most cases the hiring has been a good match, and, when it is not, the new teacher leaves for another school within the first 2 years.

The Right Leg: Collegiality

Unlike most schools, the faculty room is a delightful place to hang out. I hear and see positive interactions among staff—the easy laughter, the positive conversations about kids, the sharing of ideas. This is more than the congeniality of peers who like each other, which they do; it is the collegiality of professionals who respect each other and support each other to do what is best for their students.

I have talked with most of the teachers. They feel that they have truly chosen education as their career. Several started in other careers (law, business) and switched to teaching. The principal talked with me about the ability of the teachers "to see what's in it for kids and go after it with a vengeance." This requires a principal who works with the staff and is good at getting teachers what they need to get the job done; the current principal does this well and is appreciated by the staff. As I walk through classrooms, I observe teachers walking through also, talking about students and sharing ideas and teaching strategies.

The Left Leg: Professionalism

There may have been a time when Campbell Union School District was doing little professional development, but no more. No district within our region is doing more to guarantee that all teachers are implementing best practices in literacy than Campbell. Late afternoons, weekends, and summer days see rooms full of teachers learning best practice from trained professionals who are also experienced Campbell staff. Expert and peer coaching to support implementation of these practices are built into professional development activities.

When I talk with and observe teachers at Rosemary, I see consistent use of these best practices. What I also see, and teachers have commented on this to me, is continuity from classroom to classroom. Teachers are aware that what they are doing is building on what previous teachers did and will be built on by what future teachers do. Thus, the intellectual stimulation that results from collegiality and quality professional development, and the respect and voice in one's work life that comes from working with peers and administrators who respect you, leads to increased job satisfaction. These characteristics of a professional working environment are all an integral part of the Rosemary way.

Teachers feel heard and respected by their principal and by the district office. The union representative told me that at the monthly union meetings, when reps from other schools raise school concerns, she very seldom has any issues to share.

Most telling is a comment from one experienced teacher about her experiences at Rosemary. When she started teaching many years ago, one veteran teacher approached her regularly and served as her mentor. Although her mentor retired several years ago, this teacher feels that she still looks over her shoulder for her mentor's support and approval. More important, this teacher now seeks out beginning teachers at Rosemary and volunteers to be their mentor. As she said to me, "This is the Rosemary way, and I feel responsible to carry on the tradition." Several other teachers who were part of this conversation agreed. Two teachers new to Rosemary shared how supportive they find the experienced teachers to be, and how different this is from the previous schools in which they have taught.

Over the last few years, San Jose State University (SJSU) has developed a collaborative working relationship with Campbell schools. Field placements in three preservice credential programs (concurrent multisubject/learning handicapped, 20% intern CLAD, and 100% intern) occur at Rosemary. SJSU offers support for the district program for beginning teachers. In addition, four Rosemary staff members are enrolled in the Teacher Leadership Program, a school-based, action-research centered, MA program designed for teacher teams interested in becoming more effective school leaders without necessarily earning an administrative credential. I coordinate this master's program.

The Arms: Managing and Leading Change

Change is clearly part of the Rosemary way, particularly change that is focused on doing what is right for students. When I asked teachers why the school was perceived to be special, they were not sure how to answer. Most often, I heard about the great kids and parents; the trust, congeniality, and collegiality among staff; the caring for the students; and caring about what's happening in each other's lives. Neither Harriet nor current teachers talk about the commanding presence of a long-term respected principal or a few teachers who led and enforced the Rosemary way. Yet, it is as Harriet says, "When teachers come, they don't do their thing. They do Rosemary's thing." The Rosemary thing means doing what is best for kids, and when that means change in current practice, then the Rosemary way is to change.

The Heart: Resiliency

If I heard one message most consistently that accounts for the deep commitment these teachers have to Rosemary and its students, it is that each teacher has chosen to teach at Rosemary knowing that the student population is the most needy of any of the schools in Campbell. They sense that what they do every day is important, that the students need them, that the students and parents truly appreciate the teachers, that the smallest recognition is really appreciated by the students.

I had hoped to learn how Rosemary has stayed focused on doing what is best for students for so long. The answer is neither simple nor exportable. I think that the main lesson is that the elements of a resilient learning community are deeply enmeshed in the culture of Rosemary School; that is, each student and each adult feels cared about, knows that the expectations are high and the support is strong and that his or her participation is valued by the community.

This is a school where I would happily send my grandchildren.

Student Outcomes

Campbell Union School District assesses student progress based on district standards. At least 51% of all students in grades 2-8 are expected to score at or above the 50th percentile on the California Achievement Test (CAT) 5 for reading, language, and math; Spanish-speaking limited-English proficient (LEP) students are assessed on the Spanish Assessment of Basic Education (SABE) 2. Clear minimal expectations by grade level have been set for district-developed assessments in reading, writing, and mathematics. Data are reported by school and by grade within school for the CAT 5 and for the district assessment, with a composite score reported that indicates the percentage of students at each school by grade level who meet or exceed district standards. Rosemary staff use these data to make decisions about instructional practices. In addition, teacher judgment is a critical voice in decision making at Rosemary.

District Standards

Fifty-one percent of Rosemary students meet or exceed the district standards for reading/language arts, and 55% meet or exceed the district standards for mathematics. Results for Spanish-speaking LEP students are impressive—60% meet or exceed district standards for reading/language arts and 50% meet or exceed district standards for mathematics.

Teacher Judgment

The clear focus for Rosemary School and Campbell Union School District overall is to have all students reading at grade level by the end of grade 3. Books have been leveled, and teachers do regular alternate rankings of students to determine which students are at or above grade level, which students are making good progress and will reach grade level, and which students need increased support. The Rosemary principal reviews the alternate rankings with each teacher in grades K-3, and helps the teacher plan for the increased support needed.

As I sat writing this section, I spent a half hour on the phone talking with the principal. She had recently completed the teacher conferences involved in this process and was not only able to tell me the number of students in each class who needed additional support, but talked with me at some length about the special circumstances of many individual children to explain to me how the process works. It is clear that teachers and the principal know students and their work well, and that the principal knows the teachers and their work well.

Other Related Student Data

The attendance rate at Rosemary is 95%, slightly above the district average. The student suspension rate is noticeably below the district average.

Rosemary School
401 West Hamilton Avenue
Campbell, CA 95008
408-364-4254

Chapter 3

What's In It for Me?

A nurturing school climate has the power to overcome incredible risk factors in the lives of children. What is far less acknowledged is that creating this climate for students necessitates creating this environment for all school personnel.

Benard (1993, p. 48)

Resiliency is about building a community that is rich in the protective factors of caring, high expectations, purposeful support, and ongoing opportunities for participation. To accomplish this, it is important that we adults support our own resilience; we need these protective factors too.

> **Examine your own resiliency. When and how have you overcome adversity? Who and what helped you? What strengths did you gain?**

What's in it for me, whether I am a teacher, an administrator, a parent, a student, a grandparent, a school board member, a community member, is the opportunity to help build a community, with and for my neighbors and for myself, that is rich in the protective factors so that we all can have a more hopeful future. I am a teacher; I was an administrator; I am a parent; I like to think that I am always a student; I am a grandparent; I sit on several boards; I am a community member. I want to live in a place where people care about each other, where expectations and support are high, and where participation is valued. I want this in my home, in my workplace, and in the community where I live.

This must include taking care of myself. For the 14 years I was a high school principal, I worked very hard to build a resilient community for students, staff, and parents; I did this before I knew what resiliency theory was. At the same time, I never found time for lunch; I exercised irregularly; I found too little time for my wife; and I found little time for myself. What's in it for me is to continue receiving the good feelings that come with giving, but also to do some receiving as well. For educators to build a school culture that fosters resiliency, we must create the conditions for ourselves as well as for students. For adults to be effective, we too need to love well, work well, play well, and expect well.

If I am a professional educator working at a school rich in the protective factors of resiliency, the following benefits will be at the core of the school culture.

Collegiality

> I think that the problem of how to change things from "I" to "we," of how to bring a good measure of collegiality and relatedness to adults who work in schools, is one that belongs on the national agenda of school improvement—at the top. It belongs at the top because the relationships among adults in schools are the basis, the precondition, the sine qua non that allow, energize, and sustain all other attempts at school improvement. Unless adults talk with one another, observe one another, and help one another, very little will change.
>
> —*Barth (1991, p. 32)*

What kind of support do you expect from people you work with? How well do you know the work of people you work with? How well do they know your work?

Bring a group of educators into a room for a professional development activity, and you cannot shut them up. They do not want to listen to a presentation. They want to talk with each other! Why? Because teachers and administrators have very little time to engage other adults in meaningful conversation. Teachers and administrators have little expectation and little time to share ideas, successes, or concerns with each other. Practice is very private.

An important part of building a resilient school community is to create the time and expectation for teachers and administrators as professionals to be with other teachers and administrators to know each other and their work well. True professionals share practice and generate much of their own knowledge base; engineers do this; doctors do this, lawyers do this.

Professional development should be based on teachers sharing their work and the work of their students. Teachers need to watch each other teach, serve as peer coaches, develop curriculum together, plan instruction together, assess student work together, and engage in collaborative action research. Teachers should work together to develop expectations for what every student needs to know and design multiple assessment strategies to help demonstrate when students are meeting school standards and to guide strategies for helping students who are not.

Parents, community members, students, and classified staff (often left out, valuable members of the school community) also should work to be involved with the school professionals, sharing concerns and expertise, getting to know each other and their work well. This involves school professionals truly getting to know and understand the cultures that exist within the communities we serve.

Intellectual Stimulation

> What do you do to build professional relationships? Do you enjoy "talking shop"? Does such talk help make you more effective? Whom do you work with who challenges you to think about what you do?

In a school rich in protective factors, adults challenge each other to be reflective, to share ideas, to ask good questions, to read widely, to think deeply. Adults challenge each other to know each student and his or her work well and, just as important, to know each adult and his or her work well.

If the primary purpose of schooling is, as Ted Sizer (1985) says, to learn to use your mind well, then it must start with school professionals. Few of us have had school experience in using our minds well. Few of us have developed the habits of mind that I would put as the focus for student learning. Even with my Phi Beta Kappa key, as a student I was expected to do very little serious, rigorous work until graduate school. I became proficient at memorizing and giving back to the teacher what had been lectured to me. How can we ask students to do that which we cannot? Debbie Meier (1995) offers the Meier mandate:

> No school shall have graduation requirements that cannot be met by every professional working in the school, and therefore these requirements shall be phased in only as fast as the school can bring its staff up to the standards it requires of its students. (p. 183)

Respect

Do you feel respected by the people you work for and with? How do they show you respect or lack of respect? Do you respect these people? How do you show them respect or lack of respect?

Most schools are not very respectful places:

- Teachers and classified staff do not feel respected by students, administrators, parents, or the community.
- Students do not feel respected by most adults in school and, for the most part, do not feel respected by the community and at times not by their parents.
- Parents do not feel respected by school personnel and too often do not feel respected by their own children.
- Principals do not feel respected by most teachers, students, parents, and district office personnel.

In a resilient learning community, the culture of the school is built on respect. If teachers and administrators know each other and their work well, if students, classified staff, parents, and community members know that they are valued as participants in the school, if the conditions are in place to support students learning to use their minds and hearts well, if students and their work are known well, school personnel will feel recognized as professionals, parents will feel recognized as collaborators, and students will feel recognized as the central focus of the school.

Voice

> Do you feel listened to at work? Who values your opinion? How do they show you? Do you value what others have to say? How do you let them know?

It is unlikely that any school will foster resiliency unless the members of that school community have significant voice in the workings of that community. This is particularly true for teachers. Teachers currently have the traditional voice in their classrooms that comes with the privacy of practice that results when a teacher shuts the classroom door. They should also have voice in the work of peers that comes from knowing colleagues and their work well. Teachers are professionals, and professionals should have collaborative say over their work lives. When teachers know that their voices are valued in the daily workings of the school, they are much more open to the voices of students, parents, classified staff, and community members.

Increased Job Satisfaction

> What and who brings you joy at work? What do you do to build these people and these activities into your daily work life?

When teachers and administrators work to know students and student work well, when they commit to help every student learn to use his or her mind and heart well, the conversation changes. You no longer hear bad-mouthing of parents and students. You no longer hear bad-mouthing of peers and administrators. As the protective factors of resiliency become central to a school community for the children and the adults, you can see, hear, feel, taste, and smell the difference in a school. You see teachers and administrators engaging peers, students, parents, classified staff, and the community in the support of student learning. You hear decisions being made based on what is best for students, based on consideration of the needs of individual students. You feel the satisfaction that teachers sense when talking about how rewarding it is to work with their students because the students are growing and are appreciative, as are the parents, the principal, and the community. You can almost taste and smell the satisfaction when members of the school community repeat Maria's words, "They really trust me here."

Obstacles

In my opinion, the key obstacles to creating resilient learning communities are

1. deeply held beliefs and practices that indicate that not all students are believed capable of using their minds and hearts well;
2. schools that are too large to support knowing each student well;
3. schools that are too large to support teachers, staff, administrators, and parents knowing each other well;
4. lack of time for professional educators to know each other and their work well;
5. lack of time for professional educators to know students well;
6. popular public belief that public schools are failing and that the solution is outside of the school—top-down solutions.

Deeply Held Beliefs

If you use the following questions to assess your school, particularly if you insist on specific evidence, you will learn a lot about the belief system that guides the daily practices of the school.

- How successful is your school in meeting the needs of your students?
- Which students are you doing an excellent job for? Which students could you serve better?
- What specific evidence do you have to support your answers to these two questions?
- What is blocking your school from being more successful?
- What are the underlying beliefs of your school culture that support these blocks?
- What needs to change for your school to be more successful?
- What specific evidence do you have to support your answers to these last three questions?

All important school redesign efforts should begin with a serious study of the underlying beliefs of the staff, parents, and students. If we do not believe deep in our hearts that all students are capable of learning to use their minds and hearts well, meaningful school change will not occur and last. Often, change efforts start with a mission statement, arrived at by broad-based consensus. What I am proposing requires a much more in-depth look at beliefs and practices. Answering the questions above, particularly seeking a wide variety of evidence to back up your answers, will require honesty and usually a fundamental change in expectations for students and oneself. Collecting evidence is discussed in Chapter 7.

Many current school practices and circumstances indicate that we do not believe that all students are capable:

- Some of these school practices—ability grouping in particular—are sacred to many parents and to many teachers. Yet, tracking students by ability sends a very clear message to students that rigorous study is available to and expected of only the select few. Tracking is discussed in more detail in Chapter 5.

• We are still in a world that too often discourages females and students of color from taking certain "demanding" courses.

• Assessment practices at many schools are based primarily on norm-referenced tests, objective tests made by teachers, and subjective teacher judgment. Results from norm-referenced tests can offer valuable information about school effectiveness and are important to our publics. If we really value students using their minds and hearts well, however, we need to assess their ability to do so. Assessment practices at each of the schools described in this book balance standardized test results, performance-based student assessment measures, and teacher judgment.

Thus, truly looking at, questioning, and changing one's deeply held beliefs are the most difficult obstacles to overcome because they reflect so clearly on what we expect from ourselves, as well as from our students.

School Size

• **What percentage of the students at your school does the principal know by name?**
• **What percentage of the students do most teachers know by name?**
• **What percentage of the teachers and classified staff do all teachers and classified staff know by name?**

The school size issue is heavily ingrained. Athletic, music, and advanced placement programs all potentially very valuable for helping certain students learn to use their minds and hearts well, are based on having a large student population to select from. Yet, the success of Central Park East Secondary School in East Harlem, a school with 450 students in grades 7 to 12, where fewer than 5% of the students drop out and more than 90% of graduates go on to and succeed in college, and the success of numerous other small schools in New York City and elsewhere attest to the power of small schools (Klonsky, 1996; Lee & Smith, 1994; Meier, 1995). Debbie Meier writes that "large schools neither nourish the spirit nor educate the mind; . . . what big schools do is remind most of us that we don't count for a lot. . . . Small school size is not only a good idea but an absolute prerequisite for qualitative change in deep-seated habits" (p. 107).

The most important prerequisite for developing a resilient learning community is the underlying belief in each child's ability. The second most important prerequisite is to know each child and his or her work well. When both of these are in place, every child can be viewed as the responsibility of every person at the school. If I could recommend only one change that I think is most crucial to improve the quality of learning for our students, especially those students in urban schools, it would be to reconstitute schools so that the maximum enrollment at any school does not exceed 500 students.

Time

Time is without a doubt the most valuable resource for school improvement. Thoughtfulness is time-consuming; collaboration is time-consuming.

Look at how time is used at your school:

- **How engaging are staff meetings at your school? Leadership team meetings? Home and school club meetings? Professional development activities?**
- **How much time do teachers spend working with individual students or students in small groups, really getting to know students and their work well?**
- **How much time do teachers spend working with other teachers in small groups, really getting to know teachers and their work well?**

School leaders should remember that every time they gather people for a meeting, they are modeling teaching behavior. If school leaders choose to run meetings from the front of the room consistently, the message to teachers is that teacher-led, whole-group instruction is okay. If school leaders choose to give information at meetings consistently, the message to teachers is that information giving is okay as the primary teaching strategy. Good leaders model desired behaviors at every opportunity.

Resilient school communities set aside time for students and staff to know each other well. A strong student advisory program, such as at Anzar (Chapter 1) and Moss Landing Middle School (Chapter 4), allows teachers and students to work together on school issues and for an adult and a small number of students to get to know each other over several years. At a large senior or junior high school, with large class sizes and 6-, 7-, or 8-period days, an advisory period may be seen as one more responsibility on top of dealing with 15-plus students per day. Many middle and high schools are changing the way they use school time, however, with the result being that teachers teach fewer students. See "Personalizing Schools" in Chapter 5 for more details.

Many schools use professional development days, up to 8 per year in California, or schedule a weekly time when students start school late or leave early for staff to work together. Too often, these days are not focused, and teachers attend with minimal expectations. We have learned what "best practice" is for professional development (University-School Support for Educational Reform, 1997), however, and, in schools like those described in this book, where time is used to look at student work and at student needs and to get to know each other's work well, time used productively pays off in student learning.

Popular Beliefs and Simple Solutions to Complex Problems

The popular, and perhaps true, perception that many public schools, particularly inner-city schools, are failing has led many people to question the role of public schools. Should schools teach only "basic academic skills," and if so which ones, or should a school try to protect students from many of the societal problems that they bring to the school? Is it the school's responsibility to teach driver's education, AIDS prevention, smoking cessation, conflict resolution, critical thinking, music, art, vocational skills . . . ? What should be on this list and who should decide are at the forefront of the educational agenda for most states and our nation. The result is a top-down approach, stressing national standards and perhaps national testing, and if not national, then at least state standards and state testing.

Many educators, myself included, believe very strongly that the top-down approach undermines school improvement efforts, has little positive effect on student learning, and will probably speed the movement to finance private schools of choice publicly. Long lists of what every student should know and tests that objectively measure this will not lead to schools knowing students well and challenging students to use their minds and hearts well. It will lead to teaching to the test. When I was in 9th and 10th grade, living in New York state, I took New York Regents Exams. My world history teacher finished lecturing from the textbook in January, and we took practice exams for the second half of the course. I did very well on the exam, forgot a lot of facts the day after, and left the class with little appreciation for the importance of history.

Real improvement will come when a community agrees that every student is capable of using his or her mind and heart well, that the protective factors of resiliency are needed by all students and adults, and commits to making this happen. Beware of simple fixes for complex problems! Creating resilient learning communities is not a simple fix!

What Does It Look Like?

The next three chapters describe what schools look like that are caring, have high expectations and purposeful support, and value participation. I cannot offer a simple list of things that will make a school more caring and three for high expectations and three for participation. Building a resilient learning community is about deeply held beliefs, school culture, and daily practice. Much needs to change if schools are to foster resiliency. The case studies at the end of each chapter in this book describe schools that I believe are centered on fostering resiliency in students. You read about Anzar High School and Rosemary School. In this chapter, you will read about Cesar Chavez School.

After reading the next three chapters, you should be able to answer the following questions:

- **What does a school look like whose culture is centered on the principles of resiliency?**
- **What would curriculum, instruction, and assessment be like in a school that is designed to foster resiliency for all students?**
- **How would teacher and administrator roles change in such a school?**

Why Me?

We all make compromises in our lives that help us cope with the obstacles that confront us. We also decide what is worth fighting for. Whenever any of us compromises on our commitment to the youth of our community, the future for our youth becomes less hopeful. All youth—all people—need the protective factors of resiliency in our lives. We need them in our family, community, and school.

Ted Sizer (1985, 1992) does an excellent job of describing the compromises made by Horace, a hypothetical fine high school English teacher, and the ways that Horace comes to grips with these compromises and works to uncompromise.

What Do I Do First?

Chapter 7 deals with the issues of change. You can start with the following steps, however:

1. Self-assess: Assess and challenge your own deeply held beliefs about whether you believe in your head and in your heart that all students are capable of using their minds and hearts well. Assess and question your deeply held beliefs about how you learn. Collect real evidence to back up your initial thoughts on this.

2. Talk, talk, talk: Hold "essential conversations" with whomever will reflect with you. As you challenge your deeply held beliefs, ask hard questions of yourself and your friends. Ask hard questions within your family, community, and school. Require evidence when people make definitive statements. The more you talk and listen, the clearer your own belief system will become.

3. Read, read, read: The references at the end of this book offer numerous suggestions for books and articles you can read that will challenge your belief system. Pass the readings on.

4. Talk some more: Keep the essential conversations alive.

5. Prepare to lead: Do not allow the typical compromises that educators, students, parents, and the community make because of lack of will to occur within your family, community, and schools. Read Chapter 7.

Will There Be Public Schools in the 21st Century?

I have heard that 6 out of 10 parents would send kids to private schools if they had the money to do so. Even though voucher initiatives have failed at the polls in several states, the concept of schools of choice is still commonly heard in the media and in election campaigns. Yet, quality public schooling is at the heart of a democracy. Every child, regardless of wealth, race, ethnicity, sex, religion, handicap, sexual preference, or primary language, deserves the opportunity to learn to use his or her mind and heart well.

Public schools will be preserved as a cornerstone of U.S. democracy if citizens like us assess, question, and adjust our deeply held beliefs about the purpose of schooling and work to build resilient learning communities that we come to know well. Ownership creates responsibility, commitment, and hopefulness.

Cesar Chavez School

I began seeing a high percentage of our students dropping out when they reached middle school and high school. Their Spanish was bad, and their English worse.

—Andy Dias, Bilingual Resource teacher

Seventy-five percent of our fifth graders were not on grade level. It didn't matter if it was the students in our bilingual or SDAIE (Specially Designed Academic Instruction in English) classes. The turnover rate at Chavez is very large. About 54% of our fifth graders were not here in first grade.

—Ida Larsen, Reading Recovery Resource teacher

Our goal is biliteracy for all students. Academics is only a part of it. We really want to see loving people, productive, creative members of society.

—Andy Dias

A School Snapshot

I began working with the principal and several teacher leaders at Cesar Chavez in the spring of 1996. We examined the school culture and looked for ways to build a more resilient learning community for students and staff. Teacher leaders and the principal were passionately committed to improving the literacy of their students. Their single-minded focus impressed me.

The teacher leaders asked me to spend time at the school trying to understand why student outcomes were not improving more rapidly. Most teachers had been attending a variety of literacy trainings, and discussions in the faculty room and in staff meetings often focused on implementing the strategies taught in the trainings. After talking with many staff members and observing in classrooms, I suggested that there was little coherence to what teachers were doing. Almost all teachers were trying to implement new literacy strategies. Each teacher was doing it in his or her own way, however. There was little coordination, no peer or expert coaching, and no accountability system in place to support the implementation of new teaching strategies.

They decided to address these issues with the full faculty at an upcoming professional development day. As a result of their facilitation, all faculty

- Agreed on five reading and four writing best practices
- Agreed to focus instruction on these best practices
- Using their lesson plan books for the previous 2 weeks, listed activities they had implemented that fit under each of the best practices
- Highlighted which best practices they felt most competent with and which they felt least competent with
- Paired off with another teacher who felt competent in areas the teacher felt less competent in
- Agreed to peer coach with the second teacher, with a focus on the strategies highlighted

I attended a faculty meeting the following week and introduced the staff to peer coaching, including several role-play situations. The next week, every teacher was given release time to peer coach and to be peer coached, including preconference, classroom observations, and postconference. During the subsequent week, I attended a second faculty meeting to give the faculty an opportunity to talk about the peer coaching experience, to role-play the pre- and postconferences, and to set an agenda for peer coaching for the next school year.

Background Information

Cesar Chavez School is located in one of the poorest neighborhoods in East San Jose. The school enrollment is 836—84% Hispanic; 11% Asian; 3% White, not Hispanic; 2% other. Sixty-five percent of the students are English-language-learning students. Ninety-one percent receive free or reduced price lunches.

Due to substantial enrollment growth (666 in 1996-97 to 836 in 1997-98) and the California Class Size Reduction Program, Chavez hired 6 new teachers in January 1997 and 11 new teachers for 1997-98. Thus, at the beginning of 1997-98, 17 of the 40 teachers were new to Chavez. In addition, the principal resigned during the summer of 1997, and the Title VII coordinator was appointed to be the new principal.

In fall 1997, the new district superintendent told each school to adopt a formal literacy program and make it the focus of their school literacy plan. Schools did not all need to choose the same program. The Cesar Chavez faculty decided, with superintendent approval, to focus their plan on the nine literacy strategies rather than adopting a formal literacy program. Through a competitive, in-district grant program, Chavez was one of five Alum Rock schools awarded $88,000 to support implementation. The money was used to hire a part-time teacher to work with kindergarten students who are limited in both their primary and their secondary languages, a part-time teacher to work through the school parent center to offer parenting and ESL classes, and a teacher to work with fourth and fifth graders who are below grade level in English reading. Money was also used to purchase books and printers to support instruction. In addition, Chavez received a grant of $50,000 from the Community Foundation to support literacy and money from the Noyce Foundation to train two teachers to be Reading Recovery teachers.

Several important components of the literacy plan were already in place. There were four Reading Recovery teachers to work with primary-grade students as a safety net. Considerable money had been used to purchase instructional materials. Also, the Parent Institute for Quality Education had conducted 12-week parent education classes twice in the previous year, enrolling more than 200 Chavez parents.

Staff members say that 1995-97 was spent learning literacy strategies and purchasing appropriate instructional materials; 1997-98 was the year to build in the necessary support to assure implementation.

A Second School Snapshot

Throughout the 1997-98 school year, 15 teachers, grades K-3, participated in an Early Literacy Inservice Course (ELIC) taught by one of the Chavez teachers and funded by the school district. In addition to serving as the instructor, this teacher worked with each of the 15 teachers as an expert coach and demonstration teacher. The 15 teachers were a mix of new and experienced staff. In addition, seven non-ELIC teachers, one paraprofessional, and the principal attended another early literacy program, California Early Literacy Learning (CELL). Three other teachers were receiving the intensive Reading Recovery training. Thus, 27 staff members were involved in literacy training.

In January 1998, the staff were surveyed to learn if the nine literacy strategies were being used consistently by teachers. Responses indicated that implementation was inconsistent for many teachers. I was asked to return to the school to meet with three teacher leaders and the principal. We agreed that 1) additional peer coaching training and support were necessary; 2) peer coaching should focus on the strategies most appropriate at particular grade levels; 3) the leadership team needed to take on the role of "cheerleading squad," encouraging and reinforcing teachers as they implemented literacy strategies and as they peer coached; and 4) a system needed to be put in place so that the principal could more easily monitor implementation of the strategies. From January to May, I met with the staff four times to facilitate peer coaching. On a voluntary basis, most of the staff paired off and conducted peer coaching cycles during the winter and spring.

As a part of our planning, the school leadership team and principal agreed that an accountability system was necessary. All teachers were suppose to do an "alternative ranking" of their students based on running records three times per year. These rankings were turned into the principal. Teachers were also to use this information to meet in grade-level teams to plan support for all targeted students. The leadership team developed a form to support this process, and the principal agreed to hold teachers accountable for implementing the grade-level literacy strategies, for conducting the running records, and for developing and implementing a plan for each targeted student. Baseline data, using running records of district and school benchmark books, for all grades were established in February 1998.

Uniqueness of the School

What happens for a staff when it accepts the collaborative responsibility to help every student be literate and to create a resilient learning community that supports students and teachers in this effort? I have visited Cesar Chavez many times. I have talked with teachers and students. I have walked and driven through the neighborhood. If the staff at Chavez did not foster resiliency for each other, I do not know how they can come to work every day and care so deeply about children whose needs are so great.

Below, I intersperse a few of my observations with many quotes I have gathered from conversations with Chavez teachers.

Collegiality

This is my second year as a teacher. There is a very apparent and deep commitment amongst the veteran teachers to the literacy of kids. They are the models for what is expected of the newer teachers. This commitment and support from other teachers and administrators really makes a difference for me. They think nothing of providing suggestions, ideas, materials, and support—anything I might need to facilitate lessons and to accomplish my job as best as I can.

We are good friends at this school. Many of us earned our bilingual credentials together in college and were hired together. Unlike my husband, who also teaches, the people I work with are my friends who I call on the weekend.

When I came to this school from another district, I got a lot of support from other teachers. Teachers at Chavez support each other and are focused in a common direction. There is none of the bicker-ing that occurred at my previous school.

Anytime I have visited Chavez, whether I sit in the faculty room, in the office, in staff meetings, or in school leadership team meetings, I am impressed by the positive talk about students and by the sup-port, laughter, and joy these teachers find in working together.

Intellectual Stimulation

One of the things that makes the profession attractive to me is that I've had plenty of opportunities for professional development. I like going to school, and I value the opportunity to learn to benefit my students and me. I've been teaching for 27 years, and I still get involved in school leadership and in student study teams so that I get information that I can use with my kids.

One of the reasons we have that sense of professionalism is that, even before we developed site-based leadership, José (Garcia, the principal) encouraged teachers to attend whatever conferences they requested.

Not a lot of teachers leave at 2:45. Twenty-one of the teachers have taken the whole year course in Effective First Teaching. Fifteen are currently enrolled in ELIC. There is an amazing commitment by teachers here.

Recently, I was at Chavez facilitating peer coaching training with the staff. I asked Andy Dias to observe how long it took for the staff to engage actively in the small group simulation I set up for them. Often, at the end of the school day, teachers need prompting to begin serious work. Andy's observation was that all teachers were in their groups and on task within 1 minute. This is consistent with my ob-servations over time. This staff takes professional development very seriously. Clearly, the number of teachers who voluntarily partici-pate in the variety of literacy trainings is indicative of this commitment.

Respect

We give each other room to vent and to understand each other's positions. It is the unwritten law at Chavez that we respect each other, work through issues in grade-level meetings, and not butt heads.

We have worked very hard to not have friction between lower and upper grades or between bilingual and SDAIE teachers. The leadership team has to make decisions for the whole school. We have gotten away from thinking only about our kids in our own class-rooms and instead think about the kids in the school as all of our kids. We team-teach; we switch kids around; we share lessons and materials; we plan lessons together.

It helps that we each have 8 hours of paid time for grade-level plan-ning outside of school hours.

We've always had a united staff. Regardless of who the adminis-trator was, the staff was a constant factor. Teachers either like it or they don't. The majority have stayed. And we stay in contact with those people who have left and gone on to bigger and better things. We invite them back for showers and staff parties, and they come.

Until last year when we went to 20 to 1, we have always had teach-ers with the appropriate credentials. All of the bilingual teachers were fully certified. This was very unusual and was important to our sense of professionalism.

I hear the same message from teachers at Chavez that I hear at Rosemary: "These kids need me. They appreciate me and tell me so. Their parents are so appreciative. What I do every day is important."

Voice

We have had five principals in the last 6 years, and the school has kept running itself. Schools need strong leaders, but it is better when there is strong school leadership that includes the principal, as it is now at Chavez.

Site-based management empowers teachers because we feel we are making decisions that affect students. As we make budget decisions, we build in support and resources where we see the need.

Because we support each other, people are not afraid to get in and work. Work is not the problem. It is being able to have the materials and skills to do it.

Under the leadership of former principal José Garcia, who left during the summer of 1997, and current principal Eva Ruth, formerly the bilingual resource teacher at the school and coordinator of the Title VII grant, the teacher leadership team has a major voice in school decision making. It meets at least twice a month. This leadership team consists of nine teachers and the principal. It is responsible for making many of the most important decisions facing the school. It sets the school plan and it oversees the school budget. The teacher leaders take issues to the staff at large for input and for their consensus.

Increased Job Satisfaction

You must have love for teaching based on love for the kids. I've been at Chavez for 28 years, and I can tell you that if you have that love, the rest is easy.

What attracted me to this school are the kids. They are lively and full of life. You can inspire and motivate them, open the world to them.

As an adult in the community, I see the need for every student to be literate and to think critically and analytically. The challenges they face are difficult enough that if they don't have the skills they might not make the right decisions. . . . I entered the profession for political reasons. I've always had strong feelings about minority children not doing as well in school and why. I feel that the best possible way for me to contribute at this point in my life is in the classroom. Having a male teacher may serve as a model to not follow certain paths. I hope that I offer them an alternative, especially

*for so many that do not have dads at home. That is, in fact, who I
am for many of my students. Just now, as I walked past the cafete-
ria and saw all the kids sitting together, I was reminded of why I'm
doing this.*

It is this love for children and deep caring for the future of these
children that makes Cesar Chavez such a special place. When children come from communities pervaded by poverty, the protective
factors that foster resiliency must be at the heart of the school if the
children are to have a hopeful future.

Overcoming the Obstacles

*The children are so very needy, not only academically but also in
their social life and in the community. We get them for only a few
hours a day, but we try to make this a safe place for them, a place
where they feel comfortable, a sanctuary where they can forget
what is happening at home and in the community. We want them
to feel safe, wanted, and loved.*

I know of no school staff that exudes more of an infectious and
deeply held commitment to each and every student. The school has
grown large; the number of new teachers needing support is overwhelming; there is never enough time. The staff clearly knows that
improving the literacy of the students it serves cannot be solved with
a magic wand, however. Staff has been consistent in saying to the
district that professional development must stay focused on literacy
for at least 3 to 5 years and that resources must be focused in this
direction.

Student Outcomes

Apprenda (Norm-Referenced Test Given in Spanish)

Total reading scores for 1997 were substantially higher than for
1996 in grades 1, 2, 4, and 5. For grades 2, 4, and 5, the student average scores were above the 45th percentile. Total language scores were
also higher for students in those grades. For grades 2 and 4, the student average scores were above the 50th percentile.

Stanford Achievement Test
(Norm-Referenced Test Given in English)

Scores were not as impressive on the tests in English. For all grade levels, the student averages for both total reading and total language were in the 20th and low 30th percentiles.

As stated earlier, 1997-98 is seen by staff as the first year of implementing the literacy strategies staff spent the 1995-98 years learning. We know that it takes 3 to 7 years to implement a quality literacy program successfully. Apprenda results lead me to be optimistic that over the next few years, student literacy at Cesar Chavez will improve substantially.

Cesar Chavez School
2000 Kammerer
San Jose, CA 95116
408-928-7300

Chapter 4

I Care, You Care, We All Care

But How Do Students Know That?

This place hurts my spirit.

—Poplin & Weeres (1994, p. 11)

Human relationships are the heart of schooling. The interactions that take place between students and teachers and among students are more central to student success than any method of teaching literacy, or science, or math. When powerful relationships are established between teachers and students, these relationships frequently can transcend the economic and social disadvantages that afflict communities and schools alike in inner city and rural areas.

—Cummins (1996, p. 1)

Throughout my schooling, I was motivated primarily by grades. If a teacher had told me to stick my head through a glass window to earn an A, I would have looked questioningly at the teacher and then run to the head of the line to do so. Most students are not motivated by grades, however. Most students are motivated to work in school by the relationships they establish with teachers and peers. One of the important lessons I learned as a high school teacher and principal is that the majority of students work hard for teachers they like and respect and from whom they feel respect, and they do not work hard for teachers when the student does not feel respected; and students decide very quickly if a teacher is worth working for. Thus, the heart of teaching is really about establishing bonds and relationships with students. Norm Lezin (1997), the CEO of Salz Tannery in Santa Cruz, California, says that a good school is one at which "adults are wrapped around students" because "only relationships change people."

A close bond with a competent, emotionally stable caregiver is essential in the lives of children who overcome great adversity. Emmy Werner (1996) found that after a family member, a favorite teacher is reported to be the most positive role model. Thus, it is important that teachers look for the strengths and possibilities within each child, and that means at times to look beyond the hostility in some youth to the insecurities that lie underneath. I was struck by comments made by Steve Wozniak (Wolfson & Leyba, 1997), cofounder of Apple Computer Company, regarding three heroes in his life. He listed his fourth-and fifth-grade teacher, a high school electronics teacher, and his father. The secret is to know the student well.

The words of Mervlyn Kitashima, one of Werner and Smith's (1992) resilient children are presented in Figure 4.1.

> **Shadow a student for a school day. Sit in classes, eat meals with the student, check out the restrooms, observe the peer relationships as a student does. What is it like to be a student at this school?**

In this chapter and in the next two chapters, I present brief lists of the kinds of things I look for when I visit a school. I asked friends and professional colleagues to help me develop these lists; their names are mentioned in the Acknowledgments. The lists are presented together as observational tools in Resource A. No item on these lists is sacred. The one sacred premise is the belief in the potential of all students to learn to use their minds and hearts well.

My Grandma Kahaunaele is the only person I remember who would comb my hair. I remember going to school one day and the teacher said to me, "Doesn't anybody ever comb your hair? Doesn't anybody ever wash your face?" I guess I was dirty. Grandma Kahaunaele was the only one who would comb my hair. You know, Hawaiian girls always have long hair, and I had long hair, but it was always tangled, and it was always dirty. I remember sitting in the playground, first grade, and wondering why my head was so itchy. It's because it was so dirty. Back then I'd scratch and scratch. Grandma Kahaunaele was the one who would wash my hair, and she was the only one who would take the tangles out. She would sit me down at her knee and she'd have this giant, yellow comb. She'd patiently take every tangle out of my hair. And for any of you who've had long, tangled hair, with a comb going through it, not fun, you know? Your head is yanking as it gets caught, and I'd be crying. She would say, "Almost *pau*, almost *pau*." *Pau* means finished. "Almost done." She would eventually get finished, and I remember feeling clean, and I remember feeling pretty, and I remember feeling like maybe somebody cares for me, even for just a little while.

Mervlyn was married at age 16 and had her first child at age 17. Pregnant girls were not allowed to continue at school. The dean of students went to the counselor and insisted that the counselor begin the parent/student program that they had been discussing and that Mervlyn be the first student enrolled. Incidentally, Mervlyn has been married to the same person for 26 years. Her husband is a school teacher. She is a district coordinator for the Parent-Community Networking Centers in Hawaii's Department of Education.

Figure 4.1 Excerpts from "The Faces of Resiliency" by Mervlyn Kitashima (1997), one of the participants in Emmy Werner and Ruth Smith's Study

What Does a School Whose Culture Is Centered on Caring Look Like?

Henderson and Milstein (1996) list five categories for caring under the profile of a resiliency-building school:

- Members have a sense of belonging.

- Cooperation is promoted.
- Successes are celebrated.
- Leaders spend lots of positive time with members.
- Resources are obtained with a minimum of effort.

Although I do believe that each and every school must set its own path toward fostering resiliency and that there is no formula for making this happen, I also believe that certain beliefs and practices are characteristic of schools making a sincere effort to be caring communities. These practices are clearly reflected in daily practice and in school culture; they are not something people do for 5 minutes a day to display caring. When I wrote the first draft of this chapter, I began to write long lists under each category. I realized that I was practicing what I preach against. I was writing the standards. Therefore, I have chosen to list only four items in each category. These are things I look for when I visit a school.

1. Sense of Belonging

- Students talk freely about feeling respected, supported, and known by teachers, administrators, and peers.
- Teachers and classified staff talk easily about feeling respected, supported, and known by administrators, peers, students, and parents. (Ask the custodian.)
- Office staff are friendly and courteous to students, staff, parents, the community, and visitors.
- Body language in the halls is unanxious—students are not afraid of other students; student body language does not change when adults approach.

2. Cooperation Is Promoted

- Cross-age tutoring programs are in place to support student learning.
- Cooperative learning is taught and practiced in all classes.
- Conflict resolution skills are taught and practiced throughout the school.
- Students are seen mixing easily across race, ethnicity, and gender.

17. 3 defective light bulbs out of 500 test

18. 64 germinated seeds out of 70 planter

19. According to the 1900 census, the U.
76,212,168. Find the percent of the U
in each of these states.

   a. Iowa
      2,231,853

   b. New Yor
      7,268,89

_____

20. According to the 1990 census, the U.
248,709,873. Find the percent of the
lived in each of these states.

   a. Iowa
      2,776,755

   b. New Yor
      17,990,4

_____

21. An electronic note pad originally cost
$207.20. After tax is added, the price

   a. What is the percent of discount?

   b. What is the percent of tax?

3. Successes Are Celebrated

- Students, teachers, staff, parents, and community members are recognized for their contributions in a wide variety of ways.
- People use the word "we" when talking about the school.
- Positive communications go home from teachers and administrators regularly.
- People talk openly about what didn't work and what was learned.

4. Leaders Spend Lots of Positive Time With Members

- Administrators are seen interacting with students in positive ways.
- Administrators know and use the names of all or most students.
- Teachers, students, parents, and staff talk about the principal seeming to be everywhere.
- Class does not stop when the principal walks in.

5. Resources Are Obtained With a Minimum of Effort

- The campus is clean and orderly.
- There are lots of books in classrooms.
- Teachers report that office staff are supportive of their teaching.
- The supply closet is open and copy machines are readily available.

What Are Curriculum, Instruction, and Assessment Like in a School That Is Centered on Caring?

Some people might argue that caring and respect are not the business of schools, that what we need to focus on is high academic standards that all students are held accountable for so that students will be prepared for the workforce of the 21st century. My response to this is threefold:

1. Being caring and respectful means guaranteeing as much as we can that every child can read, write, and compute.

2. Being caring and respectful means holding high expectations for every child regardless of race, ethnicity, gender, economic status, sexual preference, or learning handicap.

3. If we want children to be caring and compassionate, then we must provide schools that model caring and compassion.

Debbie Meier (1995) argues that

caring and compassion are not soft, mushy goals. They are part of the hard core of subjects we are responsible for teaching. Informed and skillful care is learned. Caring is as much cognitive as affective. The capacity to see the world as others might is central to unsentimental compassion and at the root of both intellectual skepticism and empathy. . . . There is no tolerance without respect—and no respect without knowledge. (p. 63)

Nel Noddings (1995) makes a strong case that schools should organize around themes of caring rather than around the traditional disciplines.

Again, I kept my list short to reflect the key things I look for when I visit schools.

Curriculum

- The work is meaningful to the students; students can tell you why they are doing what they are doing.
- Curriculum is integrated and thematic.
- Curriculum respects and acknowledges the ethnography and community of the students, using this as a departure point for curriculum that explores diversity of culture and opinion within and without the community.
- Students have choices in what they learn (curriculum), how they learn (instruction), and how they present what they have learned (assessment).

Instruction

- Students are working, and teachers are coaching; that is, students are actively engaged in work.

- Teachers are talking with individual students or with small groups of students.
- Students spend extended periods with the same teacher and with the same students.
- Time is provided for teachers to work together on developing instructional strategies, including peer coaching.

Assessment

- Student work is displayed throughout the school.
- Students know and can articulate expectations teachers have for student learning. Rubrics are assessable and have been developed with student input.
- Students can be seen presenting what they have learned to others.
- Students have opportunities to demonstrate what they learn in meaningful ways, including self-reflection and participation in their own performance review.

How Do Teacher and Administrator Roles Change in a School Focused on Caring?

1. *Decision Making*

- Important decisions are made in a collaborative manner, involving all stakeholders in the decisions; one seldom hears, "We can't," "We aren't allowed," "I wasn't told."
- Meetings designed to make decisions set aside adequate time for reflection, discussion, consensus building, and planning for action.
- Ground rules for decision making are agreed on, known, followed, and regularly reassessed.
- Conflict resolution strategies have been agreed on, are taught, and are practiced.

2. *Student Discipline*

- Expectations for student behavior are reasonable, positive, public, known, and enforced with consistency.

- Classroom discipline is dealt with primarily by the classroom teacher; there are very few referrals to the office for disrespect.
- The school "disciplinarian" does not spend the majority of his or her time disciplining students; rather, he or she spends considerable time working positively with teachers, students, parents, and the community.
- Student discipline is done privately, in a problem-solving mode. (At Central Park East Secondary School, the habits of mind are used in student discipline situations to focus students on solving the underlying problem.)

3. *Teacher as Adviser*

- No secondary school teacher is responsible for more than 90 students.
- A strong student advisory system is in place. Advisories will not work in schools where teachers are responsible for large numbers of students.
- Teachers maintain regular contact with parents regarding student progress, including positive feedback.
- Teachers, parents, and students collaborate to develop an individual learning plan for each student.

4. *Teacher as Collaborator*

- Teachers can be seen working in a collegial school culture—adults talk with one another, observe one another, help one another, laugh together, and celebrate together.
- Conversations in the faculty room are lively, with teachers talking positively about students, student work, their own work, and the work of colleagues.
- Faculty and staff are not seen brooding in the faculty room or in the parking lot or segregated by sex, race, department, or age.
- Time and resources are provided for teachers to collaborate.

In Conclusion

As stated in Chapter 1, resilient children usually have four attributes in common: social competence, problem-solving skills, autonomy, and sense of purpose and the future. A school that strives to be a resilient learning community builds its culture; designs curriculum, instruction, and assessment; and assigns roles and responsibilities that foster these four attributes. It is only when students and staff are known well and their work is known well that schools can truly do this.

Resilient children are very good at seeking out and recruiting substitute parents. Teachers and school administrators need to be prepared to welcome these relationships. Schools should be places in which students and adults delight in each other's company. Resilient learning communities are such places.

Moss Landing Middle School

Essential Conversations

Caring for Students

> Teachers take care of you here. If a student is a troublemaker, the teacher tries to help him. She doesn't tell the teacher at the next grade. The student does not get sent to the office every day. The teachers really try to get to know you and help you. That's why there are so few fights at this school.
>
> —*Kolin, sixth grader*

Caring for Teachers

> Because of the support and caring I got from my team members, the students never knew I was a first year teacher. I never told the kids. Developing projects as a team, with considerable time built into the school day to do so, gave me great support. Everything was well planned. I was able to be on top of things the first year because we had a program as a team. I wasn't told to open the book and teach in a rote way. Also, we have a discipline plan, and there are not enormous discipline problems. It is unusual to have this kind of support.
>
> —*Kathy Rosen, seventh-grade teacher*

Caring About Student Learning

> What impressed me when I came to the seventh-grade team
> this year is that at the first team meeting we looked at the
> entire year, dividing up projects and deciding what to do
> with the first one so that the second one would build off of
> the first, the third off of the second, etc. Student work is really
> driven by the school outcomes. All projects stress accessing
> information, communication, social responsibility, and
> problem solving. We really believe that kids need this to be
> successful. You see so much growth in the kids.
>
> —*Tom Hiltz, seventh-grade teacher*

Background Information

Moss Landing Middle School (MLMS) is located in an econom-
ically diverse, predominately rural setting in the Salinas Valley. A
country road and agricultural land form boundaries to the school.
MLMS was created in 1988 for the purpose of serving sixth, seventh,
and eight graders. Prior to that time, the district was organized
around K-8 schools and one high school. The student population is
555—43% Hispanic; 50% White, not Hispanic; 7% other. Twenty-four
percent of the students are classified as English language learners.
Fifteen percent of the students are classified as migrant. Thirty-six
percent are on free or reduced lunches. All Resource Specialist Program special education students are fully mainstreamed. English-
language-learning students are mainstreamed for at least 50% of the
school day. More than half of the teachers are conversationally fluent
in Spanish, and another third are studying to be so.

During the 1990-91 school year, more than 3,000 hours of planning time were spent by school community members writing a plan
for systemic school reform. This plan was accepted by the state department of education for a planning grant, and the 1991-92 school
year was spent designing a school action plan. MLMS was then selected to be a California Restructuring School (SB 1274 school), the
only middle school in our region chosen, and was given funding for
5 years to implement its plan.

In 1994, MLMS was selected as a California Distinguished
School. In addition, in 1996, the North Monterey County School

District was among the initial districts to join a partnership with the California State Department of Education to be a "Challenge District," setting clear high standards; adopting clear accountability measures; building partnerships with parents, businesses, and communities; and moving critical decisions to the school level.

Uniqueness of the School

> It is not so much that Moss Landing Middle School is in the middle of nowhere as that it is on the edge of everywhere.
>
> —*Cheryl Smelt, MLMS staff*

Clarity of Focus

The school community reached consensus on "essential agreements" that drive curriculum, instruction, students assessment, and the schedule (see Figure 4.2) and on four learner outcomes (accessing information, communication, social responsibility, and problem solving). As the community worked on this, it was guided by the ideal that a caring school is one that has clarity of focus centered on successful learning by all students.

Practices That Support the Focus

The schedule is designed so that teachers know students and their work well. Teachers are responsible for approximately 60 students daily. Students are enrolled in a 2-hour English/social studies core, a 2-hour math/science core, and an advisory period. For the most part, students stay together for the academic cores, which are heterogeneously grouped. The advisories are by grade level, with the teacher serving as an adviser for students he or she teaches in one of the cores. Electives are after school and voluntary. Physical education is overseen by the core teachers.

Curriculum is project based with an emphasis on studying local marine science resources in an integrated thematic manner. During one of my visits, I sat in a classroom for 10 minutes, watching students work together on a project. I began to talk with several students about their work. After listening to them for a few minutes, I said, "Well, I understand how this works for English and social studies, but how does science fit into this?" One student responded,

Assessment

- Authentic, multifaceted, integral to instruction, and reflective
- Include the use of portfolios for every student
- Viewed as an integral part of the teaching-learning experience
- A means of measuring growth
- Driven by our outcomes, Challenge Standards, District Assessment Plan, and the state frameworks
- A diagnostic tool and recording instrument that reflects authentic assessment and is driven by outcomes
- Expect students to exhibit "growth" through a variety of exhibitions
- Provide flexibility so that each grade-level member is responsible/accountable for meeting curriculum, instruction, and assessment goals

Curriculum

- Driven by our vision
- Student centered
- Use key framework/model curriculum concepts that are congruent with our vision and the Challenge Initiative
- Use themes, developed by grade levels, to tie subject areas together
- Foster positive self-concept, self-esteem, and intrinsic motivation providing MLMS students with opportunities to experience success
- Utilize community-based themes to develop grade-level projects

Instruction

- Actively engage students
- Provide classroom environments that are brain compatible with multiple intelligences, safe, productive, and nurturing
- Utilize a wide variety of instructional strategies to meet student learning needs
- Employ instructional strategies that facilitate student achievement

Figure 4.2 Moss Landing Middle School Essential Agreements

Schedule

- Designed to meet our outcomes, vision, and the Challenge Initiative
- Provide flexibility and access toward meeting the identified needs of all students
- Group teachers and students together in teams to deliver a student-centered curriculum
- Build in ongoing planning time
- Reduce staff/teacher ratio to the extent possible
- Create home room advisement periods and schedule multi-grade activities on a regular basis

---

Figure 4.2 Continued

"This is the science class." I was surprised and impressed by the depth of integration.

School benchmarks and rubrics are being used at all three grade levels to guide the design of projects and to organize the way student work is assessed. On my first visit to MLMS, as I walked into classrooms with the principal, it was clear to me based on the questions she asked that she knew the projects and knew student work. Her questions were specific to the project and she consistently asked students to reflect on their work as it related to the four learner outcomes. She also called students by their names.

Exit Interviews

At the end of eighth grade, all students give exhibitions based on their portfolios. The intent is for the student to demonstrate, using actual work, how he or she has grown over the 3 years at MLMS with regard to the four student outcomes. Students demonstrate that they have met district standards based on schoolwide rubrics posted in all classrooms. When a school cares, it has clear standards and holds students accountable to demonstrate that they have met these standards. Panels consisting of the adviser, students, parents, teachers from other schools and districts, members of the business community, and educators from other statewide programs participate in judging these interviews. How students do on these interviews is an important part of the overall school assessment plan.

Student Advisories

All students are members of an advisory team. The advisories have three primary purposes: forging a bond among a teacher and a small group of students, maintenance of the portfolio, and preparation for the exhibition. Since 1997, advisories are by grade level. Prior to this time, advisories had been multigraded. The change was made to allow for more emphasis on grade-specific issues, particularly the exhibitions for eighth graders.

Innovative Physical Education Program

All sixth graders are bused to the local YMCA swimming pool.
All seventh graders receive sailing lessons.
All eighth graders receive kayaking lessons.

Governance Is Collaborative

The School Site Council, representing teachers from each grade level, parents, students, and the principal, is the primary decision-making body overseeing the school restructuring efforts. The staff uses a consensus model to make specific decisions on curriculum, instruction, and student assessment issues at monthly faculty meetings. Many decisions are made at the Wednesday grade-level planning meetings.

Time Is Provided for Professional Collaboration

The student day runs from 7:30 a.m. to 1:45 p.m. Teachers have a common preparation time from 1:45 p.m. to 2:30 p.m. In addition, students leave at 11:45 a.m. on Wednesdays, and teachers meet in grade-level teams to plan student work.

Community Service Is Required for All Students

All student are expected to perform 9 hours of community service each quarter.

Collaborative Relationships With
Regional Resources

The school has developed a supportive working relationship with many local resources to bring additional opportunities to students. These relationships include Monterey Bay Aquarium Research Institute, Moss Landing Port Director, Elkhorn Packard Ranch Nursery, Elkhorn Native Plant Nursery, Elkhorn Slough National Estuarine Research Reserve, California State University at Monterey Bay, Watsonville Parks and Recreation (sailing), and Watsonville YMCA (swimming pool).

Student Outcomes

The school relies on triangulated data, desegregated by grade, sex, and ethnicity, as well as staff and parent input, to evaluate the effectiveness of its program and to make decisions regarding program improvement.

California Achievement Test (CAT)
5 Results

Although the school district changed standardized tests from CAT 2 to CAT 5 since this project began, and the state is requiring a different test beginning in 1998, making longitudinal comparisons difficult, the school has found some useful information. The following is based on results from 1996:

Positives: Total battery percentile scores rose from grade 6 to grade 7 to grade 8. This is true in reading and mathematics and is especially strong in science (39% in grade 6 and 53% in grade 8) and social studies (38% in grade 6 and 50% in grade 8). These results appear to support the school's integrated, thematic, project-based approach to instruction.

Concerns: Math computation skills are low. There is currently a heavy reliance on calculators. Implications for student success at the high school level are under investigation.

Grade Point Averages

The principal and teachers review student grades each grading period, subaggregating the information by ethnicity and sex, to inform practice. Advisers maintain regular communication with parents about student progress concerns.

Exit Interviews

The staff agree that the exhibitions done by all eighth graders is the most important component for program evaluation because they guide daily practice so strongly.

A final thought: I volunteered to be a substitute teacher at MLMS. I was assigned sixth-grade humanities core. It was shortly before the winter break, which was a foolish act on my part. Although initially the students were not entirely well behaved with me, when I stopped the class to talk about its behavior, taking the time to acknowledge class members and to hear their voices, the misbehavior stopped. I found the students to be respectful and caring of each other and very complementary about the respect and support they felt from their teachers and from people in the office.

Moss Landing Middle School
1815 Salinas Road
Watsonville, CA 95076
408-633-5881

Chapter 5

Providing High Expectations and Purposeful Support

It is the first day of high school chemistry. Thirty-two students wait expectantly for the teacher to speak. The teacher begins the class by saying, "This is a college prep science class. I have very high expectations. Look around you. Based on past experience, I expect that only two of you will earn As in this class. Who will that be?"

There were no As in this class. I received one of the two Bs. Let no reader think that this is what I mean by high expectations.

Introduction

> If a child trusts us and knows that we believe in him, then none of the rest of the stuff matters. We need to have a desperate desire to make sure that every child believes in himself.
>
> —*Joe Hudson, Principal of San Juan School*

Children need to be taught that strong habits of mind are something they can learn through effort. It is the lesson of the little engine that could—I think I can, I think I can, I think I can, . . . until she does.

One characteristic of a resilient learning community is that all staff take collective responsibility for student learning—no blaming parents, students, administrators, the district office, the state department of education, the taxpayers. The educational community, including students and parents, come to see all students as problem solvers, not problems to be solved. This requires taking risks with and for students, rather than labeling them at-risk. This is the challenge that is at the very center of creating resilient learning communities. We need to look every student in the eye and say, "This work is important. You can do it. I won't give up on you. I am here to support you."

Taking the Easy Way Out

Some teachers look at their student population and the socioeconomic problems they bring to school and at their own workload and expect too little of students and of themselves.

The teacher who didn't help me at all in high school . . . was my computer lit. teacher. I got As in that course. Just because he saw that I had As, and that my name was all around the school for all the "wonderful things" I do, he just automatically assumed. He didn't really pay attention to who I was. The grade I think I deserved in that class was at least a C, but I got an A just because everybody else gave me As. But everybody else gave me As because I earned them. He gave me As because he was following the crowd. He just assumed, "Yeah, well, she's a good student." And I showed up to class every day. He didn't help me at all because he didn't challenge me. Everybody else challenges me; I had to earn their grades. I didn't have to earn his grade. I just had to show up. (Nieto, 1996, p. 58)

How do students respond when they are not treated with the respect that comes from knowing them and their work well, when they are treated as if they are not capable of using their minds and hearts well? They drop out emotionally, intellectually, and physically. Ted Sizer (1996) spent a day shadowing a high school student named Martha. At the end of the day, she suddenly hissed into Sizer's ear, "I am not stupid, I am not stupid, I am not stupid" (p. 132).

How many students feel not known and stupid? Most schools as they now are constituted create anonymity and make it very difficult to create conditions where teachers know students and student work well.

> **Spend an hour talking with each of the three students you identified in Chapter 1. Does each one of these students feel known within the school? Does each one feel that his or her work is known? Does each one feel that he or she is supported to meet high expectations?**

High Expectations: Focus on Literacy

Emmy Werner (1996) found that effective reading skills by grade 4 was one of the most potent predictors of successful adult adaptation. It is certainly true that students who are not reading at grade level when they begin grade 4 typically struggle throughout the rest of their school careers.

Increasingly, many elementary schools are focusing on student literacy as their most important academic priority. For many years, academicians argued about the correct way to teach literacy. Journals are full of articles arguing that all students learn best with a program stressing skills (phonetics typically), whereas others argue for whole language (literature). We now know that best practice is a strong combination of both, and that the emphasis should vary depending on the learning needs and learning style of the individual student. Best practice is clearly based on teachers knowing individual students and their work well.

Schools striving to create the protective factors of resiliency for their students, even if they don't know about resiliency theory per se, do know that for students to be successful, they need to be literate. These schools focus time, resources, collegial support, and professional development on helping teachers obtain the skills, attitudes, and behaviors to teach literacy in a way that expects every student to be literate, and then holds teachers, administrators, parents, and students accountable to make this happen. The case study at the end of this chapter is about one such school—Stipe School.

High Expectations: Habits of Mind

Schools that expect all students to use their minds and hearts well focus on asking questions of students and adults, the answering of which requires challenging one's mind. Probably no school focuses more clearly on this than Central Park East Secondary School (CPESS). Students are consistently asked the following questions:

- Evidence: How do we know what we know?
- Viewpoint: Who's speaking?
- Connections: What causes what?
- Suppositions: How might things have been different?
- Relevance: Who cares?

To graduate from CPESS, students must complete 14 exhibitions. The above five questions are formed into a rubric for graduation committees to use as they judge student work and guide the questions committee members ask to clarify and extend the student's learning. In addition, these questions are posted in all classrooms and are at the heart of the curriculum in every class. They are used in all classrooms, in discipline conferences, and, based on my observations when I visited CPESS, by students as they talk with their peers in cooperative learning groups and with their friends in the hallways. The purposeful focus on these five questions—habits of mind—demonstrates to every student that he or she is expected to use his or her minds and hearts well, and when students demonstrate that these habits of mind are an integral part of how they think and act, they are demonstrating their abilities to do so.

Remember from Chapter 1 that Anzar High School is also guided by its habits of mind (EPERRs, Figure 1.3).

Teaching to the habits of mind requires teaching with a rigor that is both beyond that expected in most classrooms and beyond what most adults expect of themselves. It requires a fundamental change in what teachers expect of students and themselves. Habits of teaching and learning are deeply rooted. Schools will become very different institutions only if we are very serious about the need to change our fundamental expectations and if we are willing to stick with it over a long period of time.

Wouldn't it be wonderful if all school was like kindergarten? As described by Debbie Meier (1995),

> Kindergarten is the one place—maybe the last place—where teachers are expected to know children well, even if they don't hand in their homework, finish their Friday tests, or pay attention. Kindergarten teachers know children by listening and looking. They know that learning is personalized because kids are incorrigibly idiosyncratic. . . . Kindergarten teachers know that helping children learn to become more self-reliant is part of their task—starting with tying shoes and going to the bathroom. Catering to children's growing independence is a natural part of a kindergarten teacher's classroom life. This is, alas, the last time children are given independence, encouraged to make choices, and allowed to move about on their own steam. (p. 48)

What Gets in the Way?

Belief systems that suggest that using one's mind and heart well is only for certain students, and practices that reinforce this belief, must be addressed if schools are to be built around the protective factors of resiliency. The way schools track and group students by perceived abilities tells students what's expected of them. These labels become self-fulfilling prophecies for far too many of our children. Too often children see the labels as a deterrent to try. Too often, teachers use the labels as an excuse to not challenge anyone but the most motivated to use their minds and hearts well. As Debbie Meier (1995) says, children find themselves driven into dumbness by a failure to challenge their curiosity, to build on their natural drive toward competence.

It is common for children of color and of poverty to be labeled as needy and at-risk, to be placed in remedial and special education classrooms year after year, for academic expectations to be low, for few students to graduate from high school and attend college.

One might think that labeling and tracking would be most common in inner-city schools. Many of our most affluent schools define academic winners and losers through a complex tracking system, however. Students know what it means to be a red bird or a blue bird or a yellow bird. They know what it means to be in the X class, or the Y class, or the Z class. They know the difference between AP, honors, college prep, general, remedial. They also know that, for many students, where they are placed has far less to do with ability than with motivation or how actively one's parents are involved in the school. Thus, many middle-class students know that being academically challenged is optional.

Tracking is perhaps the most controversial issue for schools today. When the parents of "academic" students do not feel that their children are being appropriately challenged, they complain loudly. They have a right to complain; their children, and all students, should be intellectually challenged in school. These parents are often involved with the school through various school committees. They know and are the school board members. They are most likely to move their students to private schools. In addition, given the reality of schools today—large schools, large class sizes, privacy of teaching practice, lack of resources, poor professional development practices—the vast majority of schools and, in particular, most teachers are not prepared to challenge all their students, particularly not in a heterogeneous classroom setting. Mandating heterogeneous classes will not improve student achievement. Major systemic reform is necessary if high expectations are truly going to be the focus of schooling for all students.

What Else Gets in the Way?

Another thing that gets in the way is not practicing what we say we believe, and therefore searching for easy answers for complex problems. I offer two examples.

The first has to do with recognizing and rewarding that which we say we value. Many schools write a mission statement that includes students demonstrating their abilities to work cooperatively. Yet, when I visit schools, I notice bulletin boards recognizing "the student of the month" and "the employee of the month," both very clear statements that the work of a limited number of individuals working independently is valued. Wouldn't it be more consistent and beneficial to recognize lots of people for the work they do together toward meeting the mission of the school?

In addition, school and school district goals listed under the mission statement are usually related to academic learning. Yet, if we look at what most schools recognize most publicly, it is the athletic program and social events. Winning sports teams, cheerleaders, and dances receive far more recognition than achievements related to where students spend most of their "15,000 school hours"—in classrooms.

Second, and again tied to most school district mission and goal statements, is the stated desire for all students to be proactive problem solvers. Yet, when I visit schools, I notice that the primary instructional strategy employed in most classrooms is teacher-led instruction. The research on brain-compatible learning has become quite well-known, and yet the instructional model remains the same—"teaching as telling"—teachers working with large groups of students. The message to students is clear: I am not expected to work very hard; I just need to memorize enough to get by; my interests and my mind and, in fact, myself are not valued at this school.

Many schools claim to use site-based decision making. Yet, important decisions regarding budget, hiring, curriculum scope and sequences, textbook adoption, and the like are still made primarily by the principal or district office or by teachers privately in their classrooms. Even when teachers are collaboratively involved in some decision making, parents and students are too often left out. If students are to learn to be proactive problem solvers—to develop the habits of mind to use their minds and hearts well—the school needs to demonstrate this value in the classroom and throughout the school community.

High expectations means believing that all students are capable of using their minds and hearts well.

Fostering resiliency means that teachers are "in kids' faces," knowing them and their work well, expecting all students to meet high expectations and telling them so. As Gary Bloom, superintendent of schools for Aromas-San Juan Unified says, "Teachers need to be relentless in insuring that students follow through and experience small successes; they phone parents, they harass and harangue; they don't give up; they advocate relentlessly for students. It needs to be more work for a student to fail than it is to get on board."

Students who need academic support are accelerated (helped to catch up), rather than remediated (too often associated with falling further behind). Only when we have high expectations and purposeful support for our students will all students have a sense of the future that is optimistic and hopeful. This requires that teachers and administrators believe, say, and practice for all students: "This work is important. You can do it. I won't give up on you. I am here to support you."

Purposeful Support

> **Think about your three students. What support is in place within their school to help assure that they acquire strong habits of mind?**

It is important that purposeful support be designed very specifically to help students stay challenged to use their minds and hearts well and to provide a safety net for those students who need additional support to do so. Examples of purposeful support are found in Figure 5.1. Please do not think that having one or a few of these examples means the school is a resilient learning community. Purposeful support is important, but only one part of the protective factors. Caring, high expectations, purposeful support, and participation should pervade all aspects of the school.

What Does a School Look Like Whose Culture Is Centered on High Expectations and Purposeful Support?

- Reasonable, positive, public, known, and consistently enforced policies and procedures are in place.
- The campus is well maintained with little litter and graffiti.
- A broad range of student work is on display throughout the school.
- Every student can name at least two adults who know him or her well and his or her work well.
- The parent's role in supporting student learning is valued and supported through parent workshops, a parent library, and availability of social services support.
- Members of the community are seen supporting student learning; space and training are provided for this purpose.
- Teachers, parents, and students talk openly about the commitment of the principal and district to all students learning to use their minds and hearts well.

(text continues on p. 84)

School Policies and Procedures

- Students need clear and consistent boundaries to feel safe and secure in school. An important support structure for students is reasonable, positive, public, known, and enforced with consistency. Optimally, students are involved in drafting, evaluating, and revising these policies.

Mentoring Programs

- Big Brothers and Big Sisters: Research by the Public/Private Ventures (Butler, 1997) in Philadelphia found that kids enrolled in Big Brothers and Big Sisters were 52% less likely to skip school than a matched control group, 33% less likely to exhibit violent behavior, and 46% less likely to try drugs for the first time. Enrolled African American youth were 70% less likely to try drugs.
- School-based mentoring programs: At Anzar High School, community members support Anzar students as academic tutors and advisors for graduation exhibitions, and serve as apprenticeship mentors.
- Intergenerational support: Foster grandparents are recruited to read with elementary students; see Stipe School case study.

Academic Intervention

- Reading Recovery: An intensive one-on-one tutoring program, led by a trained certified teacher, designed for first-grade students who are not at grade level in literacy to accelerate their learning to grade level. This program, originally developed in New Zealand, is currently in use in more than 6,000 U.S. schools and has excellent evidence of effectiveness for first-grade students who take part.
- Success for All: A schoolwide reading model used in about 750 mostly inner-city elementary schools. Success for All provides curriculum reforms, professional development, and family support, in addition to one-to-one tutoring from trained certified teachers. Research shows substantial positive effects.

Academic Intervention With Mentoring

- Advancement via Individual Determination (AVID): Designed to make underrepresented students eligible for admission to 4-year colleges, AVID involves the identification of high-potential, underachieving students as they enter high school,

Figure 5.1 Examples of Purposeful Support

offering them structured, daily academic support, and mentoring if they enroll in a strong academic program. Program evaluations have been very positive— 93.8% enrolled in colleges (Swanson, 1993).

Peer Support

- Cross-age tutoring programs: One example is a "buddy read" program used by many elementary schools, where older students read with younger students on a daily basis. See Stipe School case study.

- Service learning: A second example is service learning, where older students from a middle school (Moss Landing) or high school (Anzar) spend time in elementary school classrooms tutoring younger students.

- Cooperative learning: Cooperative learning, when done well, offers many of the protective factors for all students involved. Done well is a key, however, because orchestrating cooperative learning requires considerable skill and organization on the part of the teacher and students. Research indicates that cooperative learning strategies are the single most effective school-based intervention for reducing alcohol and drug use (Wang, Haertel, & Walberg, 1995).

- Link Crew: Link Crew is a high school orientation program that trains members of the senior class to act as mentors to freshmen and new students to orient them to the school climate and culture and to provide regular support to their freshmen "crew" throughout the year. Link Crew has been implemented in more than 170 high schools.

Incentives and Mentoring

- Cabrillo Advancement Program: The story of Eugene Lang is well known. Mr. Lang returned to his alma mater in Harlem and promised to pay the college tuition of any fifth grader who stayed in school. Based on this inspiration, Cabrillo College, a 2-year public community college in Aptos, California, began in 1991 to offer a $1,000 scholarship to a limited number of sixth graders at one largely Latino middle school in the area. Since 1991, the program has spread to three other middle schools and four high schools. Students are chosen based on

Figure 5.1 Continued

an essay they write. Counselors and tutors from Cabrillo support each of the students selected. In June 1997, the first group graduated from high school. All 23 of the original group graduated from high school and went to college.

Personalizing Schools

- Small schools: In New York City, there are now more than 50 small public schools. Several may meet in the same building, usually an old school building that once housed a large comprehensive school. Central Park East Secondary School is one of these schools, as is Urban Academy, referred to in Chapter 6. Anzar is a small high school as well. I question whether a large school can be a resilient learning community. It may be an oxymoron to use the words *large school* and *resilient* in the same thought. As I wrote in Chapter 3, if I could recommend only one change that I think is crucial to improve the quality of learning for our students, especially students in urban schools, it would be to reconstitute schools so that the maximum enrollment at any school would not exceed 500 students.

- Advisories: See discussion in Chapter 3.

- Schools within a school: Breaking a school into smaller units has been a popular alternative for at least the last 30 years. Many middle schools assign students and teachers to families, in which students stay together for all classes and teachers are responsible for fewer students. At the high school level, smaller units are often centered around career themes, and the programs are called academies.

- Core classes: If a middle or high school teacher is with the same group of students for more than one class—English/social studies or math/science are typical—that teacher is responsible for fewer students and therefore should get to know students better. Of course, it is important that the teacher be prepared in any curriculum areas taught.

- Block scheduling: In several hundred high schools across the country, classes are taught for extended periods of time each day so that students are enrolled in fewer classes per semester and teachers are responsible for fewer students. The logic is the same as for core classes.

Figure 5.1 Continued

- Staff articulate a common mission that all agree transcends personal differences.

What are Curriculum, Instruction, and Assessment Like in a School That Is Designed to Foster High Expectations and Purposeful Support for All Students?

Curriculum

- Students are actively engaged in interdisciplinary, thematic, project-based work.
- Projects have significance to students and are based on important questions raised by students, teachers, and community members.
- Curriculum respects and acknowledges the ethnography and community of the students, using this as a departure point for curriculum that explores diversity of culture and opinion within and without the community.
- Teachers individualize and modify instruction that addresses learning styles and special needs of students.
- Students comment (or proudly complain) that the work is challenging and takes time.

Instruction

- Classes are heterogeneously grouped for most of the day, with regrouping as appropriate.
- Students usually are working in small groups or independently.
- There is a well-defined safety net in place to accelerate students who are falling behind in their academic progress.
- Common instructional strategies are being used in most classrooms within and across grade levels.
- When teachers ask questions, students are required to use higher-order thinking skills to answer, and all students have equal access to respond.
- When students ask questions, teachers usually reply with a question that requires thought by the student, rather than with the answer.

Assessment

- Student learning is assessed in a variety of ways, including the use of well-publicized rubrics, public exhibitions, and self-reflection by students.
- Individual teachers use assessment strategies on a daily basis to diagnose the learning of individual students and to adjust instruction based on this assessment.
- Teachers review student work and other assessment data together to guide school and classroom practice.
- When asked, students talk articulately about their best work.

How Do Teacher and Administrator Roles Change in Such a School?

- The principal knows students and student work well and is often seen engaged in conversations with teachers about individual students and their learning.
- The principal knows students and student work well and is often seen engaged in conversations with students about their learning.
- Teachers and school and district administrators have agreed-on best practices in a limited number of areas of focus (literacy, habits of mind), and time, resources, and professional development are supporting implementation—including expert and peer coaching and collaborative action research.
- Time is provided for teachers to discuss the needs and successes of individual students.
- Time is provided for teachers to discuss classroom practice.
- Teachers talk openly about how supportive the principal and district are regarding supporting ideas and helping to provide resources.

Once again, does it matter which school a child attends? Rutter (1979) found that students do better in schools in which expectations are high. Ted Sizer (1996) presents an excellent summary of four recent research reports: Regina Kyle (1993) in Kentucky, Fred Newman and his associates (Newmann & Wehlage, 1995) at the Center of Organization and Restructuring Schools at the University of Wisconsin, Robert Felner and his associates (in press) at the University of

Illinois, and the National Center for Restructuring Education, Schools, and Teaching directed by Anne Lieberman (1995) and Linda Darling-Hammond (Darling-Hammond, Ancess, & Falk, 1995) at Columbia Teachers College. This substantial research consistently finds that the higher the level of implementation of school restructuring practices, the more positive the effects on student achievement. The restructuring strategies studied are consistent with the protective factors of resiliency.

Stipe School

A School Snapshot

During both January and May 1997, principal Kathy Harris, and resource teachers Lisa Barlesi and Neva Gazay assessed every first-, second-, and third-grade student's progress in reading using the running record procedure. Kathy then listed these students from highest performing to lowest performing by grade level and reviewed this list individually with each primary grade teacher. The September scores, collected by teachers, served as a baseline.

The January scores indicated progress and served as an opportunity for Kathy and the teachers to develop a plan for each student scoring in the lower half of the class. Also in January, the support staff (two Reading Recovery teachers, the reading academy teacher, the bilingual team teacher, the resource specialist, and the community liaison) identified specific students to work with using different safety net approaches. These included one-to-one and small group instruction, extending a student's day, modeling lessons for teachers, coteaching with teachers, peer reading partners, cross-age reading buddies, and student study team meetings with parents.

The May scores allowed Kathy and the teachers to assess how the year had gone and to make individual plans for students for the last 6 weeks of school and for the next school year. The conferences Kathy held with each teacher were not teacher evaluation conferences; they were specifically for Kathy to work collaboratively with the teacher to be sure that high expectations and purposeful support were present for every student and teacher.

Kathy knows each student at Stipe School and knows his or her work. The high expectations she has for each child are reflected in the time she personally takes to do the testing, to meet with each teacher, and to be in classrooms. The high expectations Kathy has for each teacher are reflected in the confidence she shows in each of them to support each child and in the resources she makes available for teachers to accomplish this very important task. Kathy says to students and teachers, "This work is important. You can do it. I won't give up on you. I am here to support you."

Background Information

Stipe School is one of 17 schools located within the Oak Grove School District, San Jose, California. The school enrolls 633 students, grades K-6. The student population is 52% Hispanic; 13% White, not Hispanic; 19% Asian; 8% African American; 8% other. Forty-six percent are English language learners, speaking 16 languages. Ten percent are classified migrant. Seventy-seven percent are receiving free or reduced lunches. One of the greatest challenges facing the school is the 30% mobility factor. In 1997-98, only 27 sixth graders out of 81 had attended Stipe since kindergarten.

In 1996, Oak Grove School District was among the initial districts to join a partnership with the California State Department of Education to be a Challenge District, setting clear high standards; adopting clear accountability measures; building partnerships with parents, businesses, and communities; and moving critical decisions to the school level.

Uniqueness of the School

Clarity of Focus

There is a very clear and collaborative focus on literacy in reading, writing, and mathematics. The teachers and principal have agreed on the best practices that every teacher will use at Stipe, and they have attended numerous professional development opportunities regarding these best practice. As is true at Rosemary, every teacher I interviewed seems to be motivated by the importance of his or her work and the responsiveness of students and parents. It is difficult to maintain high expectations and purposeful support without clarity of focus.

Clear Standards

Stipe staff actively participated in the district effort to develop standards in language arts and mathematics. This is consistent with the district commitment to be a California Challenge District. Teachers meet in grade-level and curricular area groups to review student work, using rubrics to assess how individual students are progressing toward these standards.

Action Research Investigations

Reviewing student data leads the staff to articulate a limited number of questions that serve as a focus of study for that year. The staff agree on a specific statement of the problem and on research questions. They then research the problem and write an action plan based on this investigation. For example, for 1997-98, staff investigate what support students need as they move from K-2 to grade 3 so that they progress from learning decoding skills to learning comprehension skills.

Purposeful Support

Three Reading Recovery teachers work with a small number of students, accelerating them to learn at or above grade level.

Schoolwide Buddy Read

For 30 minutes each day, upper-grade students read with primary grade students. The one-on-one matching stays constant for the school year.

Complex Instruction

Teachers are trained in the strategies of complex instruction developed by Elizabeth Cohen and her colleagues at Stanford University. This renowned cooperative learning program is used by teachers to support their math and science instruction.

Looping

Fifth- and sixth-grade teachers keep the same students for 2 years. This offers teachers a deeper knowledge of each student, builds trust for the teacher with both the student and the parent, and eliminates lost time at the beginning of the school year for sixth graders.

Conflict Resolution

Staff, students, and parents have received conflict resolution training. All teachers hold regular class meetings with their students. At this time, students learn and practice conflict resolution skills, including the Refusal Skills Program in grades 4-6 that teaches students the five steps to say "no" to trouble and retain their friends.

Foster Grandparent Program

Seven grandmothers volunteer 3½ hours each day to nurture and offer academic support to identified students. Three are Spanish speakers.

Motor Lab

Each K-3 bilingual Spanish student receives ½ hour per day of kinesthetic instruction. This allows the classroom teacher to do intensive interventions with five students for that ½ hour. The classroom teacher is given the time and purposeful support to work intensively with identified students.

Reading Academy and Math Club

Extended day programs offer students additional assistance.

Gifted and Talented (GATE) Program

In a weekly 2-hour pull-out program, students with different primary languages work collaboratively on research projects. Students have been involved in community service projects and in consensus building activities. English-speaking students learn Spanish as a second language; Spanish speakers continue to learn English; Vietnamese speakers learn Spanish while improving their English.

Home School Compact

Compacts defining the roles of parents, teachers, and students in achievement toward the standards are signed by the principal, teacher, parent, and student. They are translated into Spanish and Vietnamese for the language minority families.

Parent Support

The school recognizes the important role parents play in a child's learning. Three parent groups are active at Stipe, all working to further student success: the School Site Council, Comite Hispano, and the Vietnamese Parent Group. Comite Hispano has been awarded a grant by the city of San Jose to sponsor three community events that bring the neighborhood together with city agencies. Parents are regularly surveyed regarding their satisfaction with their students' education, and the results are used to guide decision making.

Shared Decision Making

Kathy is a very skilled facilitator and brings a sincere commitment to involving staff and parents in school decisions. The staff and principal have collaboratively developed a list of the decisions to be made by the principal, by the whole staff, and by grade-level teams. The staff and district have defined specific criteria for student success and, based on what every student needs to be successful, the staff and School Site Council make appropriate decisions regarding school budget expenditures. Teachers facilitate many of these meetings.

Close Relationship With
San Jose State University

Over the last 8 years, San Jose State University (SJSU) has developed a collaborative working relationship with Oak Grove schools. Field placements in three preservice credential programs (concurrent multisubject/learning handicapped, 20% intern CLAD, and 100% intern) occur at Stipe. SJSU offers support for the district program to support beginning teachers. In addition, four Stipe staff members are enrolled in the Teacher Leadership Program, a school-based, action-research-centered MA program designed for teacher teams interested in becoming more effective school leaders without necessarily earning an administrative credential. I coordinate this master's program.

Student Outcomes

Students are benchmarked using the following triangulated assessments: performance tasks in reading, writing, and math; standardized test scores on the Individual Test of Academic Skills (ITAS); and teacher judgment based on an alternate ranking system. In 1993, based on test data, Stipe staff began to focus on the writing program. A school writing scope and sequence, grade-level rubrics, and an agreed-on writing process were established. By 1996, test scores had improved markedly. In 1996, the staff agreed to focus on reading literacy. They did considerable research and extensive professional development, and designed a plan that included many of the strategies listed above. The district adopted new math materials in 1996. Despite high standardized test scores in math, the Stipe staff looked carefully at student work and data. They found that students were unable to explain clearly how they arrived at an answer on the performance math task. In the Stipe Math Action Research Plan, the teachers agreed to revisit and revise grade-level expectations and devised a simple graphic format of sequential curriculum across all grades.

January 1998 Assessments

The goal is for all students to be reading at grade level by the end of third grade. Based on running records, at mid-year 1997-98, 71% of third graders were reading at grade level, including 70% of the Hispanic students. Additionally, 44 of 52 third graders who were at Stipe as first graders were reading at grade level, whereas only 5 of 14 third graders new to the school as third graders were at grade level. This says very positive things about the Stipe program. The results on the Improving American Schools Act writing assessment were much less positive, however. Staff have been revisiting how they teach comprehension and writing based on these results.

Over the last 2 years, the kindergarten program has changed substantially, such that the literacy strategies are well implemented now. Based on running records, at mid-year, 67% of the students were reading at grade level; this was true for boys and girls and across languages. In September, 48 of 76 kindergartners knew fewer than 10 letters of the alphabet; in January, this was true for only 8 of the students.

The way in which staff at Stipe use student data and student work to guide practice, and the way they study best practice through collaborative action research, are a big part of why Stipe is such a special school for students. As principal Kathy Harris said to the staff after reviewing the January results, "The million-dollar question is, what will change instructionally in your classroom based on this benchmark? If nothing changes, neither will the results."

Stipe School
5000 Lyng Drive
San Jose, CA 95111
408-227-7332

Chapter 6

Valuing Meaningful
Student Participation

When one has no stake in the way things are, when one's needs or opinions are provided no forum, when one sees oneself as the object of unilateral actions, it takes no particular wisdom to suggest that one would rather be elsewhere.

—*Sarason, 1990, p. 83*

Stated in a more positive way:

When people have an opportunity to participate in decisions and shape strategies that vitally affect them, they will develop a sense of ownership in what they have determined and commitment to seeing that the decisions are sound and the strategies are useful, effective and carried out. This theory is basic to a democratic society.

—*Burns & Lofquist, 1996, p. 10*

> Think about your high school years. What are your most powerful and valuable memories? It doesn't matter whether these are positive or negative. You should have several examples in mind. Eliminate any that involve athletics, the fine and performing arts, school leadership activities, and school social life. Focus only on memories from academic classes. Next, and harder to do, eliminate the memory if it is primarily associated with the charisma of the teacher. Write down whatever you still have in mind.

Given the constraints I placed on you, it is likely that you have few if any memories to write down. You may remember a field trip or the learning that followed the death of a fellow student or public figure. Most likely you remember little that was directly part of the academic curriculum in high school. If I do not place these limitations on you, however, you probably have a flood of memories, many deeply felt and often reminisced about, that are of great significance to you.

I have asked hundreds of people to do this task. Typically, in a group of 30, no more than 5 have anything written down. Yet all 30 have vivid memories of participating in sports or marching band, of dances, of attending sporting events and pep rallies, of laughing about the idiosyncrasies of particular teachers and fellow students, of being laughed at or excluded by fellow students. No wonder so many taxpayers are hesitant to vote for additional taxes for schools. Their memories indicate that what they learned in classrooms was not particularly important to their lives. Most people do not feel that the academics of school actively engaged them or challenged them to use their minds well. Most people feel that the academics of school were "done to them" with little consideration for their interests and with little knowledge of who they were as people.

Participation as the
Third Protective Factor

> Talk with your three students again. How engaged are they in what happens in their classes and in the life of the school? What influence do they feel they have on the school?

> Talk with three teachers and three classified staff members. How engaged do they feel they are in what happens in the life of the school? Talk with the principal. How engaged is the principal in what happens in classrooms and in the district? What influence do these teachers, classified staff, and principal feel they have on the school?

The need to have control over one's life, to participate in how one spends one's days, is a fundamental human need. The challenge for a school that is striving to foster resiliency is to engage all students in powerful learning activities and in meaningful roles while helping them build the skills necessary to succeed at these activities and roles. This does not and should not require special programs or elaborate elective classes. It does require that teachers know students and their work well. It does require that the teacher allow students to be the workers and the teacher to be "the guide on the side" rather than "the sage on the stage." Basic skills are not neglected in such a school. Basic skills are learned because they are needed to deal with the issues and projects that form the core of the instructional program. All students are expected and purposefully supported to participate in these learning experiences.

Returning to Bonnie Benard's (1991, p. 48) quote that opens Chapter 3, we can create this kind of school if and only if the practices we want for the students are also in place for the adults. Thus, the principal must value the active participation of teachers, parents, classified staff, the community, and students in meaningful ways in the workings of the school. Going one step further, the superintendent and school board must model this behavior and value the meaningful participation of site administrators, teachers, parents, classified staff, the community, and students in meaningful ways in the workings of the individual schools and the district as a whole. The climate and culture established by district leadership play a major role in determining the climate and culture of individual schools.

What Does a School Look Like Whose Culture Is Centered on Meaningful Participation by All Students?

Ann Cook, the director of Urban Academy, a small public high school in New York City, designed the physical environment of the school to encourage, almost require, that students and teachers participate together in daily dialogue outside the classroom. All teachers share a common faculty office. Their desks are in close proximity to one another, and, as a result, teachers are often talking about school practices. Student lockers are located in this faculty office or in the adjoining room, causing students to be present for many of these discussions. This was a premeditated decision designed to encourage just such interactions. For schools to be successful, teachers must have the opportunity to talk regularly. If students are to learn to use their minds well, they need to be engaged in listening to and participating in discussions with adults that require and model the mind being used well.

Souhegan High School in Amherst, New Hampshire, is governed by a leadership council composed of a majority of students. The council consists of approximately 2 administrators, 10 teachers, 10 parents, and 30 students. Half of the students are elected by their peers, and half are appointed through a recruitment and application process designed to assure that a wide range of student groups is represented on the council. When I visited Souhegan in spring 1997, Principal Bob Mackin said that he had never overridden a decision of the council, even when the council voted for a new bell schedule that the faculty was divided over.

What follows are things that I look for when I visit a school. Many of the items included in Chapter 4 or Chapter 5 could fit here as well; several are repeated. In fact, many of the ideas listed in Chapter 5 as support, for example tutoring, are appropriate here as valued participation, for example, the value for the tutor. As in the previous chapters, no item on this list is sacred. The one sacred premise remains the belief in the potential of all students to learn the habits of mind to use their minds and hearts well. Building a resilient learning community requires major shifts in the belief systems, culture, and daily practice of most schools; this is not an easy fix.

- Students are working in the library, computer lab, laboratories, and hallways, individually and collaboratively with peers.
- Students are engaged in *required helpfulness.*
- Older students are seen working with younger students.
- Students are engaged with peers as peer helpers, conflict resolvers, and tutors.

- Students spend time each week in service learning projects on and off campus.
- Class meetings and schoolwide forums are held regularly to gather student input regarding meaningful school issues. These meetings are often facilitated by students.
- An effort is being made to include all student groups in the daily life of the school; students are not seen on the fringes of the school campus, alienated and voicing displeasure with the school, staff, and peers.
- A large percentage of the students participate in and lead a wide range of school activities.
- Signs on campus encourage students to join activities and do not indicate hurdles to complete; the words "students must" do not appear on school postings.
- Time is provided at least weekly for teachers to work together on curriculum, instruction, and assessment.
- Most students, faculty, and staff are known and welcomed by name, and many parents and community members are known and welcomed by name.
- Drugs, alcohol, smoking, and fighting infractions are statistically small and show an annual decrease.

What Are Curriculum, Instruction, and Assessment Like in a School That Is Designed to Foster Meaningful Participation by All Students?

Curriculum

- Curriculum is project based, set around complex issues, some of which relate to school and community issues.
- Students have choices in the specifics of what they investigate, how they do the investigation, and how they demonstrate what they have learned.
- Service learning is a part of every student's academic program.

Instruction

- Teachers ask students questions that require students to do critical, reflective thinking, that is, the questions associated with Anzar and Central Park East Secondary School's habits of mind.

- Teachers spend much of their time coaching students, and students spend much of their time working individually and in small groups.
- Students are usually not sitting in desks in rows.
- Students are not seen sitting unengaged in the back of classrooms.
- School resources are readily available; computers and resource materials are easy for students to access.

Student Assessment

- Students exhibit and reflect on what they have learned.
- Standards for quality work are well-known and often designed with student input.
- Teachers use student work to guide classroom and school practices.

How Do Teacher and Administrator Roles Change in Such a School?

- Principals, teachers, students, parents, community members, and classified staff are engaged in schoolwide decision making around issues of substance, including establishing school priorities, budgeting to support those priorities, and hiring personnel.
- Norms for decision making, consensus building, and conflict resolution are mutually agreed on, followed, and regularly reassessed.
- Meetings focus on meaningful input and decision making rather than information giving; agendas are posted with opportunities for agenda input; relevant information is provided ahead of meetings; participants are at meetings on time; meetings start on time and end on time.
- Divergent thinking is encouraged and heard in formal meetings and in informal conversations.
- Put-downs, side conversations, and comments that indicate exclusion are not heard in or out of meetings.

- Mistakes are celebrated as learning experiences, and responsibility for mistakes is shared without blame.
- Teachers work collegially, sharing curriculum and instructional strategies, talking about students and student work, coaching each other to be more effective. Time and resources are provided to support this.
- Teachers talk freely about feeling valued by administrators, parents, and students as participants in the whole school community.
- Administrators, faculty, classified staff, students, and parents seem to enjoy being together; across roles, people seek each other out, talk together, laugh together.
- Faculty and staff are not seen brooding in the faculty room or in the parking lot.
- Students are given classroom and schoolwide responsibilities of increasing importance with age.

Homestead High School

A School Snapshot

(Note how the examples in each of the three school snapshots demonstrate a commitment to active student participation in their learning and in the life of the school.)

At the beginning of the 1996-97 school year, business owners located in the Homestead High School (HHS) vicinity complained to the Fremont Union High School District School Board about student littering and behavior during the lunch hour. HHS is an open campus, allowing students to leave the campus during the lunch break. At a board meeting in December attended by student leaders, the school board suggested that students attempt to solve this problem prior to the board taking any action regarding closing the campus.

Student leaders welcomed this opportunity to address an issue of importance to themselves and to the student body. To gather information and understand the issues that upset the merchants, students sponsored an open forum at a restaurant in a nearby shopping center. Invitations were delivered to students, parents, merchants, staff, community members, and law enforcement officials. Approximately 100 people attended. Following the forum, student leaders identified five major problems: littering, lack of courtesy, drug use/sale, loitering, and smoking. The principal stated that drugs and smoking were administrative issues, but the other three should be addressed by the students.

Student leaders decided that the first step was to inform the student body of the problem. They knew that the vast majority of the students behaved in an acceptable manner during lunch, and that the behavior of a small minority of students might lead to loss of the open campus, a beloved privilege. Four student-led rallies were held to discuss the existing problem with students. A student who was respected by the students responsible for the problem volunteered to be one of the presenters. Law enforcement officials were also asked to explain the problem and the calls they received. The rallies were well received by students.

Next, student leaders, with the principal's support, closed the campus for 2 weeks. The purpose of this was to twofold: to demonstrate to students that a closed campus was a real possibility and to allow local businesses to feel the financial losses that would come with a closed campus. Within 2 days, local businesses called the school to voice support for continuing the open campus policy.

Third, students developed a system to monitor off-campus behavior on an ongoing basis. A flag system was instituted whereby student behavior was "graded" by fellow students, parents, and an administrator on a weekly basis. Consequences were clear. Since this system was instituted, the campus has been closed several times, but overall the behavior of students in nearby shopping centers has improved markedly.

The manner in which the school board and principal engaged students in determining and initiating solutions to a student-created problem clearly demonstrates a commitment to engage students actively in meaningful learning. Students were challenged to use their minds well, and they responded enthusiastically.

School Background Information

HHS is one of five high schools in the Fremont Union High School District. The school is located in Cupertino, California, in the heart of the Silicon Valley. The enrollment is approximately 1,800 students, 54% White, not Hispanic; 10% Hispanic; 29% Asian; 7% other, with 9.3% English-language-learning students. The school is a member of the Coalition of Essential Schools and was one of the first schools to receive funding and recognition as a lead school through the Bay Area School Reform Collaborative (Hewlett-Annenberg school reform initiative).

Study of school change began in September 1990 with common readings, speakers, and school visitations. Over the next 2 years, an increasing number of teachers exhibited enthusiasm for systemic school change. A redesign framework was written with broad input from staff, students, and parents. Interdisciplinary programs were begun that featured team teaching, project-based learning, and students exhibiting what they had learned. By 1998, approximately 40% of the students were involved in such programs sometime during their 4 years at HHS. At the same time, some teachers resisted. These teachers recruited parent and school board support for maintenance of the traditional program. Influential teachers and parents lined up on both sides of the debate. The local paper ran a series of articles about HHS's restructuring efforts. Throughout this time, the principal was clear with all parties that 1) he strongly supported and believed in the school restructuring initiative, and 2) student and parent voices should determine what percentage of the school program stayed traditional and what percentage would be designed around the initiative.

A Second Snapshot

The 1997-98 school year was spent "revisioning." The Coordinating Council, composed of teachers, classified staff, parents, and students, organized several initiatives to collect data from a wide range of constituencies to provide a basis for updating the school vision and the redesign framework. As a demonstration of commitment to student participation, 15 students were trained as facilitators and led a series of student forums. Over a 2-day period, teams of student facilitators met with 200 students, randomly selected across grade levels, in groups of 15 to 20. Students were asked three questions about how they would like HHS to be in the future: What would students be doing? What would teachers be doing? How would parents and the broader community be involved? Student responses were then reviewed and summarized by the student facilitators and other students in the leadership class. Parents and staff were also surveyed and interviewed, using the same three questions.

All results were presented to a task force of staff, students, and parents that developed recommendations and submitted them to the Coordinating Council.

I spent an hour with three of the student facilitators shortly after their meetings concluded. They showed great pride in how much the school valued student voice and in their role in helping this occur. They talked about the importance given to student voices by the Coordinating Council, the School Site Council, the Parent-Teacher-Student Association, and various school task forces. They told me that during the previous year, when teachers at HHS had supported a work-to-rule order from the teacher's union, students formed a committee to learn about the reasons and the implications for student learning; they told me how respectful teachers were of this student effort. I also sat through much of the Coordinating Council meeting that same day. It was clear that the voices of the four student members were valued.

Uniqueness of the School

Clarity of Focus

The redesign framework states,

Our goal is to improve student learning by building better connections, including:

- connections among ideas, curricular areas, and student experiences;
- connections among people in the Homestead community, including students, staff, parents, business people;
- connections with the resources and opportunities in the world beyond the school."

In addition, the teachers working with the restructuring initiative are firmly committed to the principles of the Coalition of Essential Schools.

Integrated Studies Programs

Ninth- and tenth-grade students can choose to enroll in a foundation integrated studies program that involves instruction in English, social studies, math, science, art, and physical education. Approximately 25% choose this option each year. At the 11th- and 12th-grade level, students can choose to enroll in one of four integrated studies programs: media academy; science, technology and society; American studies; or advanced placement physics and calculus.

Transitions: An Alternate Transcript
for College Admissions

HHS, along with four other California high schools, is collaborating with the University of California and California State University admissions offices in developing and piloting an alternative school transcript to use in reviewing student applications. The transcript is based on curriculum and skills standards and an assessment rubric focused on habits of mind, knowledge, communication skills, and habits of work rather than one letter grade for a class. These standards and the assessment rubric are used within the integrated studies programs at HHS, and, in 1998, were endorsed by the full faculty of the school.

Restaurant

HHS has a program to build the skills of 10th graders who failed half or more of their classes during ninth grade. As one of their projects, these students operate an on-campus restaurant for staff and students. The restaurant is managed by Chili's Restaurant, which trains the students in the skills, attitudes, and behaviors required to be effective workers in a restaurant setting.

Service Learning

All students enrolled in any of the 11th- and 12th-grade integrated studies programs are required to participate in formalized service learning or internship experiences.

School Governance

Students participate in a wide variety of schoolwide governance activities. In addition to the ones mentioned above, students serve on the Administrative Leadership Team, meeting weekly with the principal, assistant principals, teacher association representative, and classified association representative.

Student Outcomes: A Third Snapshot

Student Conferences

As a result of the conferences, students have a sense of owner-ship over their work and learning. Students are better able to articulate what is expected of them. They talk articulately and sometimes eloquently about their work. This is something they've never been asked to do before. (Lauri Steel, teacher)

In 1997-98, all students enrolled in the 9th- and 10th-grade inte-grated studies program prepared a portfolio of their work in the four areas listed above under the Transitions Project—habits of mind, knowledge, communication skills, and habits of work. They wrote essays regarding their strengths and areas for growth for each of the four areas, and in November and December presented their work to their parents and teachers at conferences facilitated by the students. This is a powerful example of student voice in curriculum and in-struction at HHS.

I watched the videotape that was made of the conferences. The tape consists of one simulated conference viewed by all students in preparation for leading the conferences and two actual conferences. I was particularly impressed when one student said to her mother and teacher, "There are some things I need to work on. I need to learn to work in groups better. Second, I need to accept critiques from my peers better. Third, I need to work on my communication skills."

Attendance

Students enrolled in the 9th- and 10th-grade integrated studies program attend school more regularly than students enrolled in the traditional program. This is true for overall attendance and is par-ticularly true for the percentage of students with five or more ab-sences—12% integrated studies versus 20% traditional at grade 9, and 10% integrated studies versus 16% traditional for grade 10.

Referrals for Inappropriate Behavior

At the ninth grade, there were far fewer behavioral referrals for students enrolled in the integrated studies program than for students enrolled in the traditional program—75% of ninth-grade students enrolled in the integrated studies program had no referrals compared to fewer than 50% of traditional students with no referrals.

Teacher Comments

I teach the Advanced Placement English class like a college class. Students who have come through the integrated studies programs are more willing to seek answers; the traditional students have trouble doing this. Their study skills and writing skills are about the same. The traditional students are better at tearing things apart; they classify very well. But the integrated studies students are better at seeing the broader picture. (Debbie Padilla, AP English teacher)

Integrated studies students are more comfortable with themselves. They are more outspoken and quicker to ask for help and to say when they don't understand something. They are more likely to see interdisciplinary connections. This is great for Socratic seminars. For me as a teacher, I find these students very comfortable to be with and easier to form an honest relationship with. (Daniella Duran, science, technology, and society teacher)

A Final Word

It may be an oxymoron that any large comprehensive high school can be a resilient learning community. Many members of the HHS community are fighting the good fight. In the spring of 1998, David Payne, the principal since 1991, left to pursue other professional interests. At the time of this writing, it is unclear whether the initiatives begun will continue with the same passionate support from the new administration.

Homestead High School
21370 Homestead Road
Cupertino, CA 95014-0292
408-522-2500

Chapter 7

Managing Change

*On Your Mark, Get Set,
Are You Ready to Go?*

One of the central lessons we think we have learned about previous rounds of innovation is that they failed because they didn't get at fundamental, underlying, systemic features of school life: they didn't change the behaviors, norms, and beliefs of practitioners. Consequently, these reforms ended up being grafted on to existing practices, and they were greatly modified, if not fully overcome, by those practices.

—*Evans, 1996, p. 5*

I wish that I could write this chapter as a step-by-step, easy-to-follow list of how to change your school into a resilient learning community. Unfortunately, the history of school and personal change clearly tells us that such rationalistic approaches ignore what it means to lead and manage change. People are far too irrational and far too comfortable with the status quo for an easy-to-follow list approach to have any positive, lasting effect on people's behaviors, norms, and beliefs. For a school to become a resilient learning community, the depth of change required in the culture of the school—in its deeply held beliefs—requires a concerted effort and commitment too deep to be addressed by a one-way-fits-all approach. It has taken me more than 50 years to reach the vision I have for public schooling. I cannot expect others to be at the same place. I must honor their journey, and I must be prepared for their questions and resistance.

> **Think of an important change that happened in your life. What caused it? How did you respond to it? What did you learn about yourself?**

What We Do Know About Change

Change is external and situational. *Transition* is the psychological process every person goes through to adjust to change and is therefore internal. Therefore, leading and managing change means working with individuals, often one person at a time, to help each person acknowledge the need for change, accept the end to the old, and begin to internalize the behaviors, norms, and beliefs that go with the new. This is particularly hard work because almost everyone would rather defend the old rather than seriously consider the new. It takes far more time than most of us recognize and are willing to give. We will continue to muddle through a range of failed school reform efforts unless we take the time to develop the skills, attitudes, and behaviors to do it right. Managing and leading change and transition requires skillful work that can be learned.

> **Managing and leading change and transition requires above all that leaders be skillful at fostering resiliency. When people know that you care about them, that you have high expectations for them and will support them, and that you value their participation, it is far more likely that they will accept change and make the necessary transitions. Please, reread this paragraph because it is so central to what this book is about.**

You are encouraged to read William Bridges's (1991) book *Managing Transitions: Making the Most of Change* and Robert Evans's (1996) book *The Human Side of School Change.*

Change starts with ourselves. The only person we can change is oneself. This is why we need to clarify our own vision and acknowledge that a vision is ever evolving. We need to work on our own behaviors, norms, and beliefs. We need to practice good listening skills actively. We need to be courageous. We need to be sure that we—you and I—truly believe in the ability of all students to learn the habits of mind needed to use their minds and hearts well.

School culture is largely determined by career teachers and staff. Many successful corporations were founded by individuals who established a corporate culture that became the "company way" and spent their careers building their corporations around that culture. Schools are different! School and district administrators, students, and parents come and go. The career teachers and classified staff are the constants who establish the unwritten rules for the way the school does its business. Therefore, school change involves transitions for people who have dedicated their lives to doing things a certain way. They know from experience that if they passively resist the changes desired, the change agent will probably stop pushing or leave. They also know that if they actively engage in the change efforts, the change agent will still leave, and a new change agent with a different agenda will soon be on the scene.

For most school employees, their experience with school change is negative and deeply emotional. They feel defensive or that their past efforts at reform were not successful. In either case, they are not hopeful.

Building relationships and working collaboratively with career teachers and with classified staff are among the most important skills leaders must learn and practice. I have taught new school administrators since 1991. One of the first issues they confront is how to work successfully with an experienced secretary or custodian.

Anyone and everyone can be a leader. Strong leadership and student learning are closely linked. Often, leadership is identified with a principal or superintendent. In reality, however, important leadership comes from teachers and often from classified staff, also from key parents and students. As a principal, I knew that key teacher leaders, the secretary, the custodian, and several parents had at least as much power within the school community as I did. When we worked together, good things happened. If we did not, few people followed. Enlisting, empowering, and trusting others to lead effectively is an important skill that good leaders have mastered.

What We Can Do With What We Know

Start With Yourself

Your deeply held beliefs are at the heart of who you are as an educational leader. If you believe that all students are capable of developing the habits of mind to use their minds and hearts well, you are ready to place this at the center of your vision. If you believe that the protective factors of resiliency influence students' ability to learn, you are ready to advocate for resilient learning communities. If, when people are talking with you, you are present to their ideas and concerns, you are a good listener. If you are trustworthy, you will have people willing to follow you. If you believe that everyone can be a leader, you are ready to lead. Spend time collecting data and honestly answering the questions in Figure 7.1; remember, there is space provided in Resource E for you to do this.

Essential Conversations

Helping people accept that change is necessary begins with the conversations that we have with colleagues about our deeply held beliefs and our vision for how these beliefs should be implemented. I find that many school leaders have not shared their beliefs or their vision with their colleagues. Many teachers cannot tell you what their principal feels is really important. Many teachers do not know what is important to the teacher in the next room. If we believe that all students are capable of using their minds and hearts well, then we need to believe the same for the adults in the school. Essential conversations are about challenging adults to use their minds and hearts well and to develop and use the habits of mind we want all students to develop.

Essential conversations require that leaders be reflective thinkers, active listeners, and courageous. Innovation will always encounter major resistance if implementation is defined according to only one reality, that of "the leader." Essential conversations occur when we discuss ideas and feelings that are important to us, and we truly listen to the other person. We must be open to the idea that our vision is not more correct than anyone else's. We must be sincerely open to

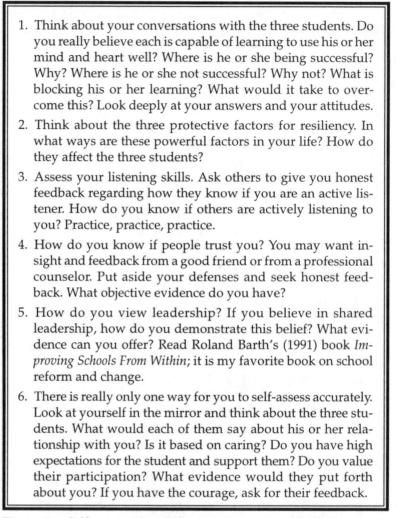

1. Think about your conversations with the three students. Do you really believe each is capable of learning to use his or her mind and heart well? Where is he or she being successful? Why? Where is he or she not successful? Why not? What is blocking his or her learning? What would it take to overcome this? Look deeply at your answers and your attitudes.

2. Think about the three protective factors for resiliency. In what ways are these powerful factors in your life? How do they affect the three students?

3. Assess your listening skills. Ask others to give you honest feedback regarding how they know if you are an active listener. How do you know if others are actively listening to you? Practice, practice, practice.

4. How do you know if people trust you? You may want insight and feedback from a good friend or from a professional counselor. Put aside your defenses and seek honest feedback. What objective evidence do you have?

5. How do you view leadership? If you believe in shared leadership, how do you demonstrate this belief? What evidence can you offer? Read Roland Barth's (1991) book *Improving Schools From Within*; it is my favorite book on school reform and change.

6. There is really only one way for you to self-assess accurately. Look at yourself in the mirror and think about the three students. What would each of them say about his or her relationship with you? Is it based on caring? Do you have high expectations for the student and support them? Do you value their participation? What evidence would they put forth about you? If you have the courage, ask for their feedback.

Figure 7.1 Self-Assess Your Behaviors, Norms, and Beliefs

questioning our vision and allowing it to evolve. Being open to sharing our beliefs, hopes, and desires with others, knowing that they may not be popular, requires that one open oneself up to one's colleagues. Very often, people will disagree vehemently with you. You need to be able to separate the intellectual discourse of your ideas from attacks on you as a person. Do not take the disagreement personally; it is seldom meant that way. In case it does get personal, stop the conversation and refocus on the ideas, not the people. This requires courage.

Essential conversations involve the exchange of ideas and the pursuit of shared goals, which, in my opinion, requires that "leaders be readers." When I walk into the office of a principal or superintendent and see only manuals on the bookshelves—no books and journals—I assume that this person is not a reader and therefore probably not a thoughtful leader. This is a stereotype, but nonetheless one I hold dear. In the very busy and stressful life that is being a school leader, you must find time to read, reflect, and converse. Reading and reflection help us form our vision. Essential conversations are required to rethink and refine our beliefs and vision, to challenge others to do the same, and to help people start to reach consensus. Being a part of essential conversations should be one of the joyful parts of the job.

In my classes for aspiring and beginning school administrators, I always begin the first few classes by asking "What's become clear since last we met?" meaning that I am really interested in their reflections. After a few weeks, I change the question to "What essential conversations are you having with your peers?" I tell them that self-reflection is not enough. If they are to be effective leaders, they must talk with people they work with. I expect them to take the ideas, discussions, and readings from class to their colleagues.

Readings to Start With

- Bonnie Benard, Debbie Meier, Ted Sizer, Roland Barth
- *Educational Leadership*, the Association for Supervision and Curriculum Development (ASCD) monthly journal
- *Horace*, a publication of the Coalition of Essential Schools
- Anything a colleague gives you to read

Support Your Own Reflection

- Set aside at least 2 hours per week for professional reading. Use this time religiously.
- Maintain a journal.
- Use a tape recorder when you drive to record thoughts.
- Join ASCD and other professional organizations. Take advantage of their resources and conferences.
- Organize a regular meeting of interested peers, within and outside your school, to reflect together. My breakfasts are quite well-known in Santa Cruz.

Practices That Support Essential Conversations

- Any time teachers come together, the focus should be on collaboration and sharing, not on information giving. Change all meetings, especially staff meetings, to reflect this.

- Circulate articles and parts of books to colleagues. Follow up with informal conversations. Keep after people so that they will expect you to talk with them about readings and ideas. Read and initiate conversation any time someone gives you something to read. Be an active listener. Be patient; it will take some people time to get involved in these conversations.

- Using the three students you have focused on, start positive conversations with other adults who know these students.

- Be courageous! Let people know that you will not participate in negative talk about students, parents, teachers, or administrators.

- Welcome opportunities to participate in conversations that focus on positive problem solving.

Assess How Well Your School Community
Fosters Resiliency

Collect data regularly and purposefully and use those data to inform and guide decision making. Collect data based on well-conceived questions. There is little reason to collect data if it is not being done with a clear purpose.

When collecting data, it is important that you look at a wide variety of school data. Always collect at least three different types of data to answer any question; this is called *triangulation*. (Reread the "Student Outcomes" sections for Rosemary, Chapter 2; Moss Landing, Chapter 4; and Stipe, Chapter 5.) As part of a leadership team, plan ways to collect data that will be meaningful to the staff and community. Engage the whole staff, parents, and students in collaborative action research—in defining the problem, defining the data to collect, collecting the data, analyzing the data, developing action plans in response to the data, and evaluating the effectiveness of the results of the action plan (Figure 7.2).

Use one or more of the instruments discussed in Figure 7.3 to assess the resiliency of your school. Gather data from a large segment of your school community. Collect these data in a variety of ways— focus groups, individual interviews, surveys, direct observation.

Background (What is the prevailing practice? What is the history of this practice?)

Problem Statement: The problem is that . . .

Purpose Statement: The purpose is to . . .

Research Questions
   1.
   2.
   3.

Data Required

Significance of This Project

Evaluation: How Will You Know If You Are More Effective?

Figure 7.2 Format for Defining An Action Research Project

In Chapters 4, 5, and 6, I offer a list of school practices that you would expect to see at a school committed to being a resilient learning community. Assess which of these are in place and effective at your school. Collect these data in a variety of ways—focus groups, individual interviews, surveys, direct observation (see Resource A for a compilation of these lists).

Look at student work for evidence. Base data collection on the following two questions: 1) What is it that we want all students to know and be able to do? 2) How are we going to know if students can do these things? Student work should always be a primary data source. Use standardized test data as one of the important data sources; your community has high expectations for how your students will perform on these tests. Make sure that other examples of student work are tied closely to students exhibiting the use of their minds and hearts, however. The case studies offer examples. Student work should be reviewed by teams of teachers, based on clear standards, and focused on question 1 above. The Coalition of Essential Schools has proposed a procedure called Tuning Protocol, which is a very useful way for teachers to do such a review of student work (Cushman, 1995).

- *Assessing School Resiliency Building,* developed by Nan Henderson and included in Henderson and Milstein (1996; see Resource B): I have used this instrument along with Bonnie Benard's (1991) article with numerous school leadership teams and with my students at San Jose State University to help them reflect on resiliency as the foundation of their own deeply held beliefs about student learning, to assess the current conditions at their school, and to develop an action plan to make the school a more resilient community for the students and adults.

- *Moving From Risk to Resiliency in Our Schools: Creating Opportunities to Learn,* developed by Bonnie Benard (see Resource C): This rubric is very easy to use and a simple way to involve people in a meaningful discussion about resiliency and the current conditions at a school.

- *Resiliency: Junior High Assessment Rubric,* developed by Cupertino Union School District (see Resource D): A district-wide task force developed a detailed rubric to assess the perception of parents and students about how well the junior high schools were meeting the needs of students.

Figure 7.3 Assessing How Well Your School Fosters Resiliency

Look at student data by subgroup, such as male/female, grade, length of time enrolled at your school, English speaker/English learner, race, ethnicity, grade. This is called *disaggregation.*

The Bay Area School Reform Collaboration (BASRC; Hewlett-Annenberg school reform initiative) has developed a rubric to be used by schools seeking membership in the BASRC collaboration. This is an excellent tool to assess your school's current status and to plan for a course of meaningful action. It can be found at http://www.wested.org/basrc.

Develop an Action Plan

Use assessment data with staff, parents, and students to reach consensus on a plan that will clearly focus on fostering resiliency for all students and adults in your school community. Do not wait until everyone buys into the vision; that will never occur, and the vision will continue to evolve over time anyway (see Figure 7.4).

- A clear belief statement focused on the protective factors of resiliency
- The givens—agreements of what is important and nonnegotiable; this could be written as a compact that participants sign, indicating agreement and commitment
- A limited number of important goal statements (three or four) that deal directly with the protective factors for students and adults
- A limited number of objectives and activities (two or three) related to each goal
- Clear ways that people will measure progress, long-term and particularly short-term, for each objective and activity; remember to triangulate and disaggregate data
- Ways to learn and celebrate as each objective and activity is completed—learn and celebrate often
- Clear agreement on how the effectiveness of the action plan will be documented
- Timeline and people responsible for leadership at each step
- Communication procedures for each step
- Timeline for revisiting, revisioning, and revising the action plan

Figure 7.4 Components of an Action Plan

Evaluate the Effectiveness of What You Do

Be honest! Collect meaningful data and share the data to make informed decisions about the effectiveness of your efforts. Data should be driven by the questions used to generate your action plan. Data should be at least triangulated, so that a variety of different types of data is collected, and disaggregated, so that you can be specific with recommendations that result from using the data to make decisions. This can be time-consuming. It can be risky if results do not support your goals, and, at times, data will not appear to support your goals.

Too often, schools do not collect meaningful data and therefore cannot demonstrate the effectiveness of good work to their various publics. Too often, we do not explain data collected in a way that the public can understand and value. In addition, we are unable to adjust our work because we don't have the accurate information needed to make purposeful decisions. Redesign efforts will not be sustained over time if we do not make good decisions based on sound data.

Understand the Importance of Transitions
and Endings

> **Think about how you handled the death of someone close to you. How did you react? What did you learn about yourself? Many people react to change in the workplace in ways similar to dealing with a death.**

Every change in an organization leads to some sort of change in the lives of the people in that organization. People lose turf, attachments, sense of future, meaning, and control. It is natural for people to wonder why there is a need for change unless what they are currently doing is inadequate, and therefore people feel criticized personally by a call for change. The more we, as leaders, understand what will change and for whom, the better we are prepared to help people with their transitions and therefore to accept endings. Leadership and management of change require that we anticipate the grieving and overreaction that comes with transitions, that we acknowledge the losses openly and sympathetically, that we communicate over and over in a wide variety of ways, that we treat the past with respect, and that we show how the endings ensure the continuity of what really matters from the past. All this is explained very well by Bridges (1991, Chapter 3).

We often think that mandating a change is enough, or explaining it is enough. Then we wonder why what we wanted was not implemented enthusiastically and sustained over time. In fact, people need to acknowledge that endings and transition to the new way of doing things have occurred. This requires changes in behaviors, norms, and beliefs. Skillful, well-planned, broad-based leadership can facilitate this process. As Evans (1996) writes, "many educational change efforts fail due to expectable problems that well-trained leaders would anticipate" (p. 4).

When I coach school leadership teams, I work with them to try to predict what every staff member would lose if the proposed changes were to occur and how each staff member is likely to behave.

Then, each member of the leadership team (typically several teachers, the principal, and sometimes classified staff) selects two or three staff members whom he or she will support through the transition process. We revisit this support effort on a regular basis. This is not manipulative and dishonest. It is important leadership in the management and leadership of change and transition.

A couple of years ago, an experienced principal I know was transferred to a different school in her district. The new school had had a series of unsuccessful principals, and she was expected to refocus the school in positive ways. She was known and respected by many of the teachers at this school. At the end of the first year, she felt that she was being successful, but also felt that some teachers were not happy with her leadership. She asked me to spend time walking around the campus talking with people, and to share with her my sense of the school climate. I spent time on the school and said to her that it seemed that her leadership had led to several teachers losing their turf. When teachers were unhappy with previous principals, they congregated in the parking lot after school to complain to each other. Now that the school was headed in a more positive direction, the leaders of the complaining had no audience. The lesson: No matter how positive and desired the change, losses occur that make the transitions difficult for some people.

Sell the Problem, Not the Solution

Meaningful change will not be implemented unless people are persuaded that there is a problem and they are involved in helping find the solution. People must be made uncomfortable with the status quo and their role in maintaining it. This should be done while helping people feel competent and hopeful to improve the situation. If teachers are made to feel incompetent, a natural reaction to being told that what they are currently doing is not working, they will resist and blame others—the students, parents, and administration—for the identified problems.

> **Think about reactions from people you know and from yourself to change. Is there blaming? At what stage? What happens to stop the blaming? Or, what should have happened to prevent blaming?**

At the same time, through essential conversations focused on students and their work, teachers and staff can be helped to accept that many of our current practices and many of our current beliefs and norms are counterproductive. Only by collaboratively accepting responsibility as a school community—teachers, staff, administrators, parents, students, and the community—for the success of all students will we truly be proud of the quality of student work.

Using student work as the focus of collaborative study encourages us to see the problem firsthand. Examine data from at least three sources (triangulation) and look at the data for specific subgroups (disaggregation).

Teachers and administrators at Mission Hill Junior High School (MHJHS) spent much of the 1990-92 school years looking at and talking about school practices and student work, reading, and visiting other schools. Survey data were gathered from students and parents. At an all-day planning session, teachers drafted a statement describing how they would like the school to be. They then graded the school against their ideal. Overall, they gave themselves a grade of D. The time taken to reflect collaboratively on the ideal versus current practices and careful facilitation by the school leadership team led the staff to agree to major redesign. The case study at the end of this chapter is about this journey. An important part of this journey is the major leadership roles played by key teachers and classified staff.

Clarity and Focus

Very often, when I am talking with a school principal, he or she will tell me about his or her vision for the school and express frustration with how few teachers have bought into it. My first question is, "If I were to ask teachers what your vision is, what would they tell me?" All too often, the principal responds, "I'm really not sure they know. I want to be collaborative and let them develop the school vision." Wrong answer!!! How can people trust you if they don't know what you stand for? The idea is not to impose your vision, but to make it an integral part of the discussion. If you want students and adults to use their minds and hearts well, you need to model this behavior publicly and often.

Teachers often see and hear a leader's vision as a series of unrelated and unimportant changes for the sake of change. Three characteristics of effective leadership are 1) the ability to create a picture of the whole that others can see, 2) consistency of support for efforts leading toward fulfillment of this whole, and 3) the willingness to protect people from other changes that are irrelevant to the effort.

At the same time, one's vision is ever evolving. On many occasions, often when I thought my vision was clearest, someone has asked me a question that either I could not answer or that gave me new insight. Being an active listener and a collaborative problem solver allows the vision leaders bring to the school to evolve into a shared vision of the school community.

Courageous Leadership and
Courageous Followership

I have used the word *courageous* several times in this book. Taking risks with your peers, with those you supervise, and with those who supervise you takes courage. Prioritizing your time when you are already working 60-plus hours per week to read, to start essential conversations, to make fostering resiliency the passionate focus of school life, takes courage. Be courageous! Ira Chaleff (1995) has written an excellent book about courage and leadership titled *The Courageous Follower: Standing Up To and For Our Leaders.*

What Does It Take to Manage and Lead Change?

Building a resilient school community requires vision, capacity, motivation, resources, and an action plan. When any of these is missing, the change will be far less likely to be implemented successfully. Figure 7.5, developed by Sandy Williams from Escondido (CA) Union High School District, offers a model presenting the consequences of omitting key elements of school change.

Remember, change primarily is about individual people and their belief systems. As Joe McDonald (1996) says, readiness to change is much more an issue of beliefs than of having a plan laid out to implement the change.

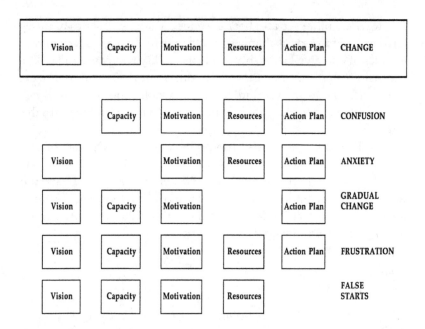

Figure 7.5. Managing Complex Change

The Section You've All Been Waiting for:
What About All the Resistance?

In my experience, there are primarily two types of resisters to change. The first are usually very vocal and often very political. They disagree with you because their deeply held beliefs are passionately held, and your vision does not seem to be compatible with their beliefs. These people are often very talented teachers who work long hours and are highly valued by students and parents. Many high school principals will talk about "their math teachers" as highly dedicated teachers who always get in the way of change. Too often, we define these people as the enemy when we should be nurturing them. They are the conscience of the school! If I cannot answer their questions to my satisfaction (probably not to their satisfaction), I am not ready to answer the questions from people interested in our re-design efforts. I learn from their questions; I need to hear their discontent; I need to not judge them because of their views but to accept their view as their valid view of their world, a world that overlaps with mine. As a principal, I spent at least as much time talking one-on-one and in small groups with these individuals as with people in favor of redesign efforts. When they got personal, I learned to stop them and to tell them that I was every bit as dedicated as they and demanded the same respect from them that they wanted from me. I valued their input, valued them as teachers, and valued them as people. When I think about the teachers I miss most from my days as a principal, it is these dedicated teachers whom I think of.

The second group can be characterized as passive–aggressive teachers who do not want to change because they have become comfortable with the compromises they have made and no longer have high expectations for themselves. Because they are less verbal, it can be harder to engage them and to know what they honestly believe. They may say they agree with the definition of the problem and even with the solutions, but they put little energy into fostering resiliency and into their teaching lives. They may be a large percentage of the teaching staff. These people were much harder for me to work with than the first group. To be successful as a leader of change and transition, you need to recognize that many of these people will transition if they see other teachers they respect doing the same first and if you are consistent with them in terms of fostering resiliency. Therefore, the member of the leadership team who agrees to work with one of these people should be respected by that person. In particular, it is important that you be clear about your high expectations and purposeful support for them. In some cases, this will have to be documented in formal evaluations. Some of these teachers will need to leave the school and perhaps the profession. Courageous leadership is critically important with this group.

A Final Word

The primary purpose of this book is to help school leaders understand and apply resiliency theory (RT) as a guide for proactive systemic school redesign. My experience in sharing RT with others is that it makes sense to people. Sharing how a resilient learning community must stress the protective factors for the adults as well as for the students is very engaging to teachers. Teachers and administrators know the many ways their school does not offer this. They are eager to share ideas with colleagues and to devote time and resources to improve the situation. I do not mean to intimate that change then becomes easy. The key underlying belief in the potential of all students is not widely supported in belief or practice. The norms and behaviors that must change to become a resilient learning community are deeply embedded in school practice. Most people would like to be part of a resilient learning community, however, and certainly want their children to attend such a school.

Several years ago, I asked a group of high school teachers and administrators to share with each other what they would show their own child at their school if their child was an eighth grader and they wanted their child to attend their high school. I had been working with this group of 25 teachers and principals for several months. We were focusing on the protective factors of resiliency as the core of their school action plan, and commitment to follow through with peers at their schools was coming slowly. Suddenly, one teacher looked at a second teacher, who was a recognized leader within our group, and said, "You do have an eighth-grade daughter. Where will she go to high school next year?" The answer was a private high school. The room became silent. Every person in that room was ashamed, for all knew that they might make the same choice. No longer was this an intellectual exercise. People got serious about developing action plans, using resiliency as the focus, that they could proudly take back to their schools to facilitate discussion and action.

Mission Hill Junior High School

This case study is longer than the previous ones. It is important to see the intricacies and stressors of the change process. You should be able to see how each of the points raised in this chapter relates to the experiences at Mission Hill Junior High School (MHJHS).

Introduction

Restructuring a school is like undertaking a major remodeling of a house. When a family has lived fairly comfortably in a house for a long time, the need for change presents itself gradually over time. The member(s) most affected by the inadequacies of the current living conditions begins to talk about change. He or she shares this vision for change with others living in the same house, hoping that the other person (people) will instantly see the same need for change that the first person has taken years to visualize clearly. Plans are drawn. Preparation for the remodeling occurs. Work begins. Everyone must give up the comfort of the old patterns. Unexpected complications cannot be predicted. Stress increases. Relationships are challenged. Interim changes have to be made that may compromise the vision.

Realizing the Need for Change

What began as individual personal and professional growth journeys for many staff members led key staff leaders to the consensus that there was a need for a new strategic plan that focused on powerful learning for all students. They realized that the existing methods of schooling were grossly inadequate.

MHJHS was a heavily tracked, departmentalized junior high school and a Distinguished California School. The school's growing population of limited-English-speaking students and special education students was segregated from the mainstream students. In spring 1991, the school district hired a new principal, the eighth principal in 12 years.

Sharing the Need for Change

Who says it's broken?!! We're a distinguished school.

Beginning in the spring of 1991, staff leaders carefully orchestrated a carefully planned effort to gain acceptance for the need to change MHJHS. The bullets that follow highlight activities of the next 12 months.

- The leadership team applied unsuccessfully for a California school restructuring planning grant.

We didn't get it, but we were committed and vowed to keep going and to reapply.

- Seventeen staff members agreed to continue studying ways to change practice at MHJHS to meet the needs of all students better.

- These teachers read, visited other schools, attended conferences together, and talked extensively among themselves.
- These teachers led a series of well-designed focus groups, looking at school performance issues with the entire staff.
- A planning team met weekly from 4 to 7 p.m. from the end of January 1992 until the end of the school year planning, developing potential implementation models for the school, and talking about ways to help each staff member make the personal transitions necessary to allow for implementation of a new model for educating students.

Envisioning a Dream House

A Pivotal Day

On February 11, 1992, at an all-school planning day, information from a student survey regarding "what is" from students' points of view was shared with staff. Students expressed feelings of alienation from staff and from each other; they felt that the curriculum was disjointed. Thus, the focus of the day was to help staff "get in touch with the disgruntled client." A new mission statement was drafted that reflected beliefs about what is best for kids and how the school must address these beliefs every day. Staff graded the school against their ideal and gave themselves a D. The question was asked if working harder would make a difference, or whether the school needed to change. A vote was taken, and more than 95% of the staff voted to make significant changes over the next 5 years.

On February 19, 22 of 27 staff members attended a voluntary meeting to do short- and long-term planning as a follow-up to the previous week's meeting. Staff agreed that "connectedness" among teachers, students, parents, community, student support services, and subject areas needed to serve as the focus for all restructuring and remodeling efforts.

On March 13, staff met all day. They agreed that certain things were to change. The school would be reorganized into teams, and a student advisory system would be implemented. Special education, limited-English-speaking, and Title I students would be mainstreamed for all core classes. Detracking would occur in academic subjects. Numerous details still needed to be worked out. The leadership team was charged with the responsibility to develop more specific plans for staff input.

Drawing the Blueprint—Gaining Building Permits

On March 25, the leadership team took a new state restructuring grant proposal to the Santa Cruz City Schools School Board. All members of the board indicated overwhelming support and approval for the breadth of the proposed changes and the innovative aspects. In addition, the remodeling of two science labs was approved by a financially strapped district.

One board member capsulated the entire board's response by stating, "This is the most positive proposal I've had to vote on since I was elected to the board."

The plan that was unanimously approved included the following:

- Grade-level academic teams
- 2-hour academic core classes (humanities and math/science)
- Student advisory program
- Heterogeneous grouping (inclusion)
- Thematic units that were integrated and interdisciplinary
- Project-based instruction
- Common preparation time for each of the four teams
- Conflict resolution program
- Seventh period selective program

Temporary Plans for the Remodel

In anticipation of restructuring for 1992-93, staff preferences were surveyed. The plan was still in need of specifics. Teams had to be formed; rooms needed to be assigned; teacher assignments had to be set. It was important to plan for support and professional development. Some took advantage; some did not. The following questions were asked:

1. Who would you feel comfortable teaming with?
2. What support do you need?
3. What training do you want?
4. What do you want to teach?
5. What are you not willing to give up?

The principal negotiated with each teacher to try to give that teacher the support and encouragement necessary to feel prepared to implement the remodeling plans. At times, this meant that those who were most supportive of the remodel were accommodated less than those who were less supportive.

The bidding began—"Who'll take Mr. X? . . . Not me, I had him last time."

The faculty voted to proceed with implementation in the fall with or without the additional state funding. In August, the funding was denied by the state.

We Didn't Get This One Either

During summer 1992, a team of 15 teachers received integrated thematic instruction training through the Bay Area Middle School (BAMS) Project. Some members from each of the four new academic teams attended. Considerable team building occurred as a result of this collaborative experience. The coordinator of BAMS was hired to coach staff in implementing integrated thematic instruction and group dynamics. Also during the summer, the school district refurbished two science classrooms to facilitate hands-on science, and a group of teachers wrote materials for the new student advisory program. In addition, the principal and library-media specialist scheduled and solicited community volunteers for the student selective program; students would be offered a broad selective program during seventh period, with minicourses offered by teacher and community volunteers.

Fall 1992—Work Begins
(Torn Up and No End in Sight)

The plan that was created by the staff and enthusiastically supported by the board was not a one-room remodel. It was a "from the ground up" renovation. Once in the middle of the renovation, many people wished they had never begun. Daily life was harder. Cooperative planning took more time. Dealing with a broader range of students was challenging. Meetings increased tenfold. Stress increased. It was hard to maintain the enthusiasm for a potentially better school.

We knew we had a good plan. We felt that we were ready. We thought we knew exactly what we were doing. Unlike the unsinkable Titanic, we had provided lifeboats; however, not everyone chose to use one.

Observations: Anticipating and Experiencing Are Two Different Things

Everyone Gave Up Something

Several teachers were teaching at new grade levels. The number of math tracks had been reduced from four to two. Science was now integrated and hands on. The variety of electives was limited, because elective teachers were needed to teach core classes. Special education and bilingual teachers were no longer teaching in self-contained programs. The Title I/bilingual coordinator was now working with the entire staff rather than with a limited number of teachers. Teachers were trying to broaden their teaching repertoires to meet the needs of heterogeneous classes of students.

Unexpected Complications

Lower than expected school enrollment led to a reduction in funds received from the district. Inadequate state funding led to a reduction in classified support staff and counselors districtwide. No state restructuring money made it even more difficult. Personal considerations prompted the assistant principal to leave for a new job mid-year. She was replaced by a retired administrator who worked part-time only.

Stress Increased

Anxieties rose, people felt overloaded, and weaknesses within the system became obvious. Like any remodel, human and materials costs were higher than anticipated and implementation took longer than anyone thought possible.

Relationships Were Challenged

The leadership team was so busy planning within its grade-level teams that it found little time to meet and coordinate as a team. All faculty were so busy working with new team members that other longstanding relationships suffered. Students complained about missing friends who were in other teams. Students talked about "good" and "bad" teams. Some parents of "gifted" academic students objected to the reduction in tracking. Parents could no longer request a particular teacher; the request needed to be for a particular team. A few parents chose to send their students to other schools. In

reality, many people who could see the need for change were so uncomfortable with the problems of the interim phase that they almost
lost sight of the goal.

Interim Changes and Doubts

"Are we sure it's going to be better?" All teachers were working so
hard that they felt dazed. Several teachers tried to renegotiate back
to the old ways. Not all teachers chose to or were able to make the
changes in teaching repertoire that would facilitate the mainstream-
ing of special needs students.

In reality, agreements and expectations were clear. Teams were
given the authority to redesign curriculum, instruction, and assessment. There was not enough training in how to do so, however, particularly, in how to do so in a collaborative process across disciplines.

"I've been teaching this way for 20 years, and it works just fine." This
is the time when it is natural to question why you ever started. The
vision has to be strong, as well as the commitment, to get through.
At the beginning of the school year, the number of Ds and Fs were at
an all-time high. Many limited-English-speaking and special day
class students were struggling so much that self-contained programs
were allowed to reconstitute on a limited basis. With responsibilities
of teams and administrators not clearly defined, student discipline
became a major concern of staff. With the resignation of the assistant
principal and the resulting extra burdens on the principal, staff questioned the leadership abilities of the principal. Teachers who had
been most supportive of change became short-tempered and emotional at meetings as a result of the additional stress. Staff leaders
were so busy in their own transition that they found little time to
support each other or staff in need.

Midway Through Year 1:
Living Through the Disruption

> Old ways of doing things are no longer appropriate, and new
> ways are not yet in place.

In January 1993, the leadership team met after having read William Bridges's (1991) book. The team was particularly struck by
Chapter 4 on the *neutral zone*. I attended this meeting and heard six
people simultaneously shout, "This is where we are now!"

Supporting the vision and each other. People continued to work longer and longer hours, attempting to make the restructuring efforts successful. When staff questioned the effectiveness of the student advisory program, the minority who wanted to disband it was outvoted. Instead, staff brainstormed ways to make it work better. The district agreed to allow MHJHS to remain onsite for planning purposes on what were suppose to be districtwide inservice days. Teachers listened to and supported each other, verbally at meetings and emotionally one on one.

Sorting and reestablishing priorities. In early May, the leadership team started to meet again. This was the first time during the school year that so many staff members had reflected as a group on how the restructuring efforts were progressing. A list was made of all teachers who were clearly "on board." There was agreement that more than 50% were committed. The leadership team made lists of long- and short-term issues. Members consistently rechecked the principal's bottom line. The principal accepted responsibility for many of the unresolved issues related to managing the transition. The principal also stated that when the leadership team made decisions and he took them to the faculty, vocal support was important; the group agreed.

Staff leaders to principal: You dropped the ball. We can't do this if you don't follow through with staff, district, and community!

Principal in response: You better be ready to back me up when I go to bat!

Recommitment to the Vision

By the end of the year everyone was exhausted. We looked like "night of the living dead," survivors of the nuclear winter.

Ten teachers and the principal carefully planned the May 14th staff development day. During the day, the bilingual teacher, who had had a very difficult year, spontaneously stood up and started a "wave" that caught on with staff and eased tensions. The staff met in small groups and celebrated the positive accomplishments of the year and made public awards of recognition to individuals for their contributions to the year. It was at this time that the staff recommitted to the restructuring effort for 1993-94, with the special note that this was only Year 1 of the 5-year plan. It was clear that the remodel was too far along to consider turning back, and that almost everyone was pleased with some parts of the remodel. In the afternoon, a barbecue was held at the principal's house.

Year 2—Best in the West

The leadership team recognized that a successful opening to the 1993-94 school year was critical to maintain teacher commitment to the restructuring efforts. At the same time, it recognized the need to begin to emerge from the neutral zone through a process that promised a higher quality of life for staff. The week of staff meetings prior to the return of students was planned carefully. A metaphor was needed to create a picture for the staff that would symbolize their work. It was agreed that this metaphor would be "best in the West." Agendas became trail guides; western music and decor set the scene; western gear was the dress code; and individual members of the staff shared the job of trail boss. These staff meetings were short, efficient, and productive. The result was a positive feeling among staff and a willingness to put extra effort into establishing a plan for positive student recognition and team recognition. For the opening district meeting, the entire staff dressed western, walked together from the school to the meeting, and sat together. The statement to the rest of the school district was clear: Mission Hill stood together with pride; Mission Hill was the best in the West.

As the second year of implementation began, the leadership team agreed on two important priorities. First, the leadership team would meet regularly with the principal. Second, emphasis would be on fine-tuning, not adding new components. The components of the plan approved by the board more than a year earlier were coming into place; everyone had a stake in implementation. Consistency of staff and program support, morale, and team building were felt to be of utmost importance.

Although the staff began the school year on an upbeat note, ongoing transition issues continued to affect morale throughout much of the school year. Resistance of a small minority of staff diminished the effectiveness of team efforts. Debates over tracking in math polarized some staff. Resistance became vocal, demanding a return to the old ways. More and more people across programs were feeling comfortable, however, and talked about the positive difference in student attitudes. The majority demanded that new and different ways be found to solve remaining issues. New focus groups were formed, and a team-oriented school planning process was designed to build cohesiveness and a common vision for the future.

The issue of advisory became a focal point for complaints. Many staff saw this as one more responsibility, with little real pay-off for students. At mid-year, advisories were dropped as a result of a staff survey. This change improved staff morale by demonstrating to staff that frustrating components of the vision could be addressed and responded to positively. Additionally, it lightened the work load and simplified the weekly schedule.

Preliminary Findings

There were indications that the changes were benefiting students. The campus was safer and cleaner. Discipline referrals were down 60%, and the suspension rate was down 70%. Graffiti on campus was sharply reduced, with only two serious cases during fall semester 1993. The academic success rate was also up, with the percentage of students passing all courses up from 75% to 85%.

Year 3—The Sky's the Limit

During Year 3, several new components were added to the vision.

- Youth Serve, a service learning program for middle school students, was introduced at MHJHS, and approximately 200 students chose service learning as their seventh-period selective.
- A technology plan was developed. The computer lab was staffed. Community partnerships were fostered. Grant opportunities were pursued, several successfully.
- Schoolwide work began on student outcomes, rubrics, and evaluation processes that could be used in all classrooms.
- The principal gave his bottom line—integrated themes must be included in all core curriculum by each academic team. At least one research report was to be integrated across disciplines each year.

Problems continued, particularly around resistance from some members of the math department, frustrations with implementation of the seventh-period selectives program, and the desire for more funding.

Year 4—Catch the Wave of Excellence—and
Year 5—Set Sail with Mission Hill

At the end of Year 3, the principal accepted a position nearer his family in Texas. His growth as a school leader and his willingness to empower staff to be leaders were central to the success of the program during the previous 3 years. The new principal, although not new to the district, needed time to understand and become part of the MHJHS way. This is a common issue in school redesign. When a person central to the vision leaves, even when he or she is replaced by a person with excellent people and management skills, as was true in this case, the vision does not belong to this new person and the transition can be difficult for all parties.

Several setbacks took place. Public and parent perception of the selective program was not positive. Teachers who had repeatedly volunteered to teach selectives during seventh period were beginning to resent those teachers who did not volunteer. By the beginning of the fourth year, the coordinators of the selective program seriously questioned their capacity to find enough volunteers to provide classes for all students. At the semester, a compromise was found that reduced the selective program to only Tuesdays and Thursdays. Second, even though the math department agreed to use a new integrated math program, one math teacher continued to teach from the traditional book instead. Third, whereas many teachers were beginning to use the new school rubrics, many others were not, and there was no accountability.

At the same time, Years 4 and 5 saw important growth in the availability and use of technology. The school was wired for technology during two net days, and considerable technology was added to the school. Training was offered to teachers, and student use of technology in support of instruction occurred schoolwide.

Year 6—Making Tracks

The original plan had been designed for 5 years. Year 6 was seen as a time to reassess. There was a general consensus that many things were going well. At the same time, it was clear to the leadership team that ownership of the school redesign was less tight than it had been in previous years. Several new staff members needed induction and support. Teachers were less consistent in enforcing schoolwide behavior expectations. A time-out room that teachers could use to deal with in-class behavior problems was eliminated for unrelated reasons, and student referrals to the assistant principal and the number of suspensions were going up.

Several important problems were identified. There was staff agreement that these problems could be addressed by giving people the opportunity to voice their concerns, that solutions could be reached by consensus, and that accountability for implementing these solutions was critical. One of these problems related to large class sizes. The superintendent agreed to give MHJHS two additional class sections for the second semester to support the instructional priorities of the school and the district.

A process was developed that would allow staff to discuss controversial issues and to reach consensus. The first topic selected was continuance of the seventh period selective program. Many staff felt that students did not use this time constructively, that community volunteers were difficult to recruit and poor at classroom management, and that perhaps it was time to return this time to regular instructional minutes. Others disagreed, feeling that students did value this time, that the selectives were important, especially for English-learning students and special education students who received tutorial support and for the many students who used the time for service learning or independent study, and that the problem was with implementation, not the concept. Students were surveyed. Results indicated strong student support.

I was asked to facilitate a staff meeting using the new consensus guidelines. Teachers in favor of the selective program did their homework. They presented the student survey results and had six students present the work they did during selective time. Prior to the meeting, they surveyed staff to understand and predict what the perceived concerns were and from whom. They came to the staff with proposals for dealing with each substantive concern. I helped the staff follow the agreed-on process. At the end of 2 hours, all but two staff members voted to continue the selective program with agreed-on modifications. Written evaluations of this meeting indicate that staff supported the process and that they wanted it used again for similar issues. I talked with several staff members 6 weeks later. They indicated that the modifications had been implemented, and that staff members were pleased with the how the selective program was progressing.

In March, the staff was presented with the results of the yearly parent survey (see "Student Outcomes," below) and with results of a related staff survey. The school vision statement, the six schoolwide student outcomes, and the 1997-98 goals were revisited in light of the data found in these two surveys. Consensus was reached on goals for 1998-99, and each staff member publicly committed to being on at least one of the task forces formed around each goal. I was present during this 3-hour meeting. The process was facilitated skillfully by the leadership team. Staff felt good about progress being made this year, were open to areas identified for improvement, and reached consensus easily about goals for the next year. I was particularly impressed by the quality and honesty of the brainstorming in evaluating the vision, student outcomes, and current-year goals and by the number of staff who were involved in planning and facilitating this process.

MHJHS was more than halfway through its 6th year of school redesign. Obviously, it has not been an easy process. Meaningful change never is. Survey results of students, parents, and staff, as well as comments from most staff, indicate a deep commitment to what is happening for students, however. Only a handful of staff would argue for a return to the old. The vast majority just wish that transition wasn't such hard work.

Background

Mission Hill Junior High School is one of two 7th- and 8th-grade schools within the Santa Cruz City School District. The enrollment is 545, 24% Hispanic; 66% White, not Hispanic; 4% African American; 4% Asian; 2% other. Ten-and-a-half percent are English language learners, speaking 11 languages other than English. Seven percent receive free or reduced-price meals.

I served as a high school principal in this district for 14 years. There has been a longstanding commitment to shared decision making and to support for school change. When I was hired in 1977, parents, students, teachers, classified staff, and administrators were on the interview panel. This practice of broad input into all hiring decisions was and still is an expectation. Each school has a budget committee consisting of teachers, classified staff, parents, and, on the secondary level, students to advise the principal. Since 1978, each school has had a school site council consisting of teachers, classified staff, parents, the principal, and, on the secondary level, students to develop and monitor a school plan for program improvement. In 1988, Santa Cruz was the first school district in the country, I think, to offer tenured teachers the option of developing their own professional development plan collaboratively with peers in lieu of formal evaluation (Krovetz & Cohick, 1993). This practice has become an increasingly popular option within numerous school districts in this region.

Student Outcomes

Parent Survey

The 1998 parent survey was compared with survey results for 1996, 1997, and 1998. Two areas of focus for the 1997-98 school year had been technology and school safety. Regarding technology, parents rated the three issues regarding technology increasingly more favorably over the 3 years—student computer proficiency, computer access, and amount of useful equipment. Regarding school safety, parents rated three issues more favorably for 1998 than for the previous 2 years—safety in school (81% satisfied), safety in classes (90% satisfied), and safety on yard (81% satisfied). Regarding the instructional program, parents were very satisfied with the science program (83%), math program (83%), and physical education program (90%), and increasingly satisfied with the humanities program (72%, up from 63% in 1996). Eighty percent of parents were satisfied with how parents were included in the school, 77% were satisfied with school spirit, and 70% were satisfied with extracurricular activities. Parents were also increasingly satisfied with school responsiveness to individual and cultural differences (73% satisfied, up from 43% in 1996). Many schools would be excited with these results and not reflect more deeply. At MHJHS, however, the voices of parents, students, and staff are relied on to guide practice.

There were several areas for concern. Parents were concerned about level of challenge (60% satisfied, down from 72% in 1996) and homework (62.5% satisfied, down from 68% in 1996). Also, parents seemed to have less understanding of the family team organizational pattern for the school (73% satisfied in 1998, down from 79% in 1996).

Parents were concerned about the selective program (57% satisfied, down from 62% in 1996) and with the availability of extra help for students (57% satisfied, down from 64% in 1996). The survey was administered prior to the adjustments in the selective program. The others areas of concern were addressed by staff in setting goals for the next year.

Results were based on responses from 173 families.

Staff Survey

All teachers were surveyed based on goals within the school plan. Results were reported for seventh-grade core teachers, eighth grade core teachers, and schoolwide elective teachers. These results were also looked at in detail in evaluating current practice and in setting priorities for the next year.

California Achievement Test (CAT) 5
(Norm-Referenced Test)

Using the results from 1996 and 1997, staff agreed that language mechanics and expression would be focus areas for the 1997-98 school year. Core teachers have increased attention to these areas. California mandated a different test for 1998, but there is a commitment to use the results from this new test to check on progress in the designated areas and to inform practice for the following year.

Final Thought

One area that the school needs to improve on is using actual student work to guide decision making. The school rubrics are available to serve as a guide. At one time, there was staff agreement that these rubrics would be used schoolwide. The rubrics need to be revisited by staff, agreements need to be recommitted to, and accountability procedures need to be put into place.

Mission Hill Junior High School
425 King Street
Santa Cruz, CA 95060
408-429-3860

Chapter 8

Commonly Asked Questions About Resiliency

(And the Answers)

$\mathbf{Q}$uestion 10: Our staff is very congenial, and we are known for how caring we are with students. Aren't we doing resiliency already?

Resiliency is not something you "do," it is something you "are." Look back at Chapter 2, particularly Figure 2.1. Your staff may care deeply, but does your staff truly believe in the ability of all students to develop the habits of mind to learn to use their hearts and minds well? Are there high expectations and purposeful support, or does caring mean that you expect less because students are so needy? How are student, staff, and community voices valued in the school? What specific evidence can you provide in answering these questions? A careful assessment of your school's practices would be informative.

Second, *congenial* means getting along well. *Collegial* is very different. Collegial refers to the ways people support each other to be more effective professionals.

Question 9: How can what happens in my classroom or in my school overcome the problems my students encounter outside of school?

You know from your own daily experiences that some of your students, not the majority, but some, who come from very troubled backgrounds are successful in school. Many others find success later in their lives. We know from Emmy Werner and Ruth Smith's (1992) research, and from our own experiences, that the student who is successful usually has known an adult who really cared about him or her, has had people hold high expectations for him or her and support him or her to meet these expectations, and has had people value his or her participation; he or she has had reason to be hopeful about his or her future. I do not mean to diminish the importance of family and community, but the basis for resiliency theory (RT) is that what you do or do not do influences the lives of your students. We all have had people enter our lives briefly who have had an influence on how we view our future. You may want to reread the inspirational words of Mervlyn Kitashima in Chapter 4.

Question 8: What is the role of the district office in fostering resiliency?

Resiliency is fostered throughout school districts when central office personnel see their primary function as supporting school efforts, as opposed to seeing school efforts supporting district initiatives. Primarily, the superintendent and other district office personnel can model behaviors that foster resiliency for the adults in the school. This includes helping the school focus on a very limited number of important priorities, including resiliency; helping to provide resources to accomplish these priorities; recognizing and rewarding collaborative efforts to accomplish these priorities; valuing student outcomes related to students using their minds and hearts well; holding school personnel accountable for helping all students achieve a limited number of important student outcomes; expecting each school community to make decisions about curriculum, budget, hiring, professional development, and so on that affect the daily workings of that school, including the participation of school people in important district decisions; making sure that all district departments and personnel respond quickly and efficiently to school requests; and maintaining good relations with the teacher and classified unions. The manner in which district office personnel interact with and respond to school personnel has a major effect on the climate of individual schools.

Question 7: How do we coach our principal so that she sees the building of a resilient learning community as a priority?

First, you need to share the ideas of resiliency with your principal. She should read Bonnie Benard's (1991) article and this book at a minimum. Second, you need to help the principal see that building a resilient learning community will further the vision and goals she has for the school. It is imperative that the principal view fostering resiliency as a critical support for her priorities. Third, you need to convince your principal that building a resilient learning community is doable for your school with existing resources and with existing staff. Fourth, you need to have the courage to help lead the effort.

Question 6: How can we create change in individual teachers about attitudes and expectations toward certain groups of students, such as Title I, English language learning, migrant, special education?

This can be difficult in many schools. Teachers are often used to these students being served in pull-out programs by specialists. They do not feel prepared to teach these students, and do not see it as their responsibility. Most research supports inclusion. Quality professional development and resource allocation support are needed to bolster this effort.

In my opinion, there are two ways to proceed. For the first option, the district, principal, or staff decides that inclusion will occur for these students and that adequate resources, especially time and professional development, are allocated to support teacher development to help assure the success of these students and these teachers. Remember that teachers need to feel successful or they will lower their expectations for students and for themselves. Therefore, high expectations and purposeful support should be high priorities for both teachers and students.

For the second option, win teachers over one at a time. You and other leaders need to share the research with individual teachers, knowing that by itself, research will not convince others. You also need to demonstrate to the teacher that, with your support, a limited number of students can be included in that teacher's classroom and that these students can be successful. You will probably need to twist arms, put your relationship on the line, and take this teacher to classrooms in which these students are being successful. You will need to share successes and strategies that have proven effective for you. You will need to take risks and to be persistent.

Question 5: How do you get a mature staff that has a history of mistrust and private practice to talk with each other about fostering resiliency?

Head on! Most certified and classified staff members want to work in a school that fosters resiliency for students, and particularly for themselves. The many compromises made over the years wear school people out. This is understandable, and not their fault! Maintain a clear focus on what is in it for staff as well as for students. In my experience, most staffs respond very positively to talk about resiliency because RT is at the heart of what most adults want in their own lives and relates so directly to why they entered teaching as a career.

Reread and follow the suggestions in Chapter 7. Mission Hill Junior High School had a mature staff with a history of mistrust and private practice. It changed because of excellent teacher, staff, and administrative leadership, careful planning, time, and patience.

Question 4: How will we know we are succeeding in fostering resiliency? What measures should we use? Who should we use them with? When should we use them?

These are important questions often asked by Emmy Werner (1996). One would expect that, if a school is increasingly fostering resiliency, students should be able to demonstrate increased social competence, problem-solving skills, autonomy, and a sense of purpose and the future. One key question then is can students graduating from your school demonstrate increasing competence in each of these four areas? To determine this, tasks should be designed, with teacher, student, and community input, for students to complete to demonstrate their competence. Students also should be held accountable to high standards of literacy and habits of mind, both of which are required to demonstrate competence in the four areas. Of course, purposeful support should be provided as needed. Reread "Graduation by Exhibition" at Anzar High School in Chapter 1.

In addition, at a minimum, schools should collect the following data:

- Standardized test score data: Whether we like these tests or not, we should expect students to demonstrate increased competence in reading, writing, and mathematics. Our public expects achievement in these areas.

- Longitudinal data: We should examine student work, attitudes and behaviors over the time the student is in a school to guide decisions about individual learning needs, as well as to determine program effectiveness. We should also conduct meaningful follow-up after the student leaves so that long-term effects can be documented and learned from.

- Survey data: Tools used initially to assess the resiliency of your school should be administered to staff, parents, and students over time to learn about perceived changes in your school's culture.

As I state in Chapter 7, school redesign efforts will not be sustained over time if we do not make good decisions based on sound data.

Question 3: Should we teach students about resiliency and help them understand how to foster resiliency in themselves?

The answer is yes, but recognize that this is not sufficient. It would be useful for students to understand resiliency and to learn ways to seek situations that foster their own resiliency. You should be building a school culture based on fostering resiliency, however, and consider teaching students about resiliency as only one of several initiatives.

Question 2: Why are you wasting our time on resiliency when our children can't read?

This commonly asked question is answered in Chapter 3:

1. Being caring and respectful means guaranteeing as much as we can that every child can read, write, and compute.

2. Being caring and respectful means holding high expectations for every child regardless of race, ethnicity, gender, economic status, sexual preference, or learning handicap.

3. If we want children to be caring and compassionate, then we must provide schools that model caring and compassion.

Resiliency and literacy are also addressed in Chapter 5 under High Expectations: Literacy.

Question 1: I am exhausted. How do I foster resiliency for myself?

This is the most common issue raised by beginning administrators in my classes. I am certainly not the best role model for this. As a high school principal and now as a university professor, I work 60-plus-hour weeks, eat on the run, and could do a much better job of caring for myself. I do have some "do as I say, not as I do" suggestions. They are listed in no particular order.

- Control your own calendar, and write in time for exercise and family on a weekly and daily basis.
- Develop a professional support group that you meet with at least every other week; breakfast meetings are easier to keep to a manageable length than end-of-day meetings.
- Recruit a mentor whom you respect to coach you through stressful times and to serve as a sounding board.
- Attend professional counseling on a regular basis.
- Write in time in your calendar to do the work-related things that bring you joy.
- Keep paper by your bed to write notes on when thoughts about school business wake you up.
- Learn to delegate properly and to trust in others to do the best they know how.
- Learn to discern what's important from what's not important. Only do things well that need to be done well. Many of the tasks given to us just need to be done or can be filed until someone reminds us to do them.
- Don't let personnel issues fester. Deal with them skillfully, now.
- Don't take attacks on your ideas personally. Relish the intellectual discourse you create, and tell people if they respond to you personally rather than to your ideas.
- Whenever you have a long weekend or vacation, leave town.

- Live near your work, otherwise you will miss dinners and events that focus on your children.
- As often as possible, say that you have a commitment that you cannot change when someone, particularly your supervisor, wants to meet with you on very short notice.
- Hold most school conversations standing.
- Be honest; it is too stressful to be someone other than yourself.

Afterword

Ending as we began:

"How do you like my school?" asked Maria.
"I'm very impressed by how friendly everyone is," said I.
"More important, they really trust me here," said Maria.

Schools that "really trust" their students–schools that value, respect, and know their students–are schools that foster resiliency for their students. Such schools are full of adults who believe that all students are capable of learning the habits of mind to use their minds and hearts well. These adults understand how important it is for student learning and for student hopefulness that all students know that they are cared about, that expectations are high, that purposeful support is in place, and that their participation is valued.

To do so, schools must also be full of adults who value, respect, and know each other well. Adults must believe that they and their colleagues are capable of learning the habits of mind to use their minds and hearts well. Resiliency factors need to be in place for the adults as well as for the students.

Few schools are full of adults who share these beliefs. Within your community and mine, however, schools are striving to be resilient learning communities. I hope that this book will encourage you to be a part of the very important work these schools are so courageously doing and to help other schools undertake their journeys.

Resource A

Observation Checklist

Caring

What does a school look like whose culture is centered on caring?

Sense of belonging

- Students talk freely about feeling respected, supported, and known by teachers, administrators, and peers.
- Teachers and classified staff talk easily about feeling respected, supported, and known by administrators, peers, students, and parents. (Ask the custodian.)
- Office staff are friendly and courteous to students, staff, parents, the community, and visitors.
- Body language in the halls is unanxious—students are not afraid of other students; student body language does not change when adults approach.

Cooperation is promoted

- Cross-age tutoring programs are in place to support student learning.
- Cooperative learning is taught and practiced in all classes.
- Conflict resolution skills are taught and practiced throughout the school.
- Students are seen mixing easily across race, ethnicity, and gender.

Successes are celebrated

- Lots of students, teachers, staff, parents, and community members are recognized for their contributions in a wide variety of ways.
- People use the word *we* when talking about the school.
- Positive communications go home from teachers and administrators regularly.
- People talk openly about what didn't work and what was learned.

Leaders spend lots of positive time with members

- Administrators are seen interacting with students in positive ways.
- Administrators know and use the names of all or most students.
- Teachers, students, parents, and staff talk about the principal seeming to be everywhere.
- Class does not stop when the principal walks in.

Resources are obtained with a minimum of effort

- The campus is clean and orderly.
- There are lots of books in classrooms.
- Teachers report that the office staff are supportive of their teaching.
- The supply closet is open and copy machines are readily available.

What are curriculum, instruction, and assessment like in a school that is centered on caring?

Curriculum

- The work is meaningful to the students; students can tell you why they are doing what they are doing.
- Curriculum is integrated and thematic.
- Curriculum respects and acknowledges the ethnography and community of the students, using this as a departure point for curriculum that explores diversity of culture and opinion within and without the community.
- Students have choices in what they learn (curriculum), how they learn (instruction), and how they present what they have learned (assessment).

Instruction

- Students are working, and teachers are coaching; that is, students are actively engaged in work.
- Teachers are talking with individual students or with small groups of students.
- Students spend extended periods with the same teacher and with the same students.
- Time is provided for teachers to work together on developing instructional strategies, including peer coaching.

Assessment

- Student work is displayed throughout the school.
- Students know and can articulate expectations teachers have for student learning. Most often rubrics are assessable and have been developed with student input.
- Students can be seen presenting what they have learned to others.
- Students have opportunities to demonstrate what they learn in meaningful ways, including self-reflection and participation in their own performance review.

How do teacher and administrator roles change in such a school focused on caring?

Decision making

- Important decisions are made in a collaborative manner, involving all stakeholders in the decisions; one seldom hears, "We can't," "We aren't allowed," "I wasn't told."
- Meetings designed to make decisions set aside adequate time for reflection, discussion, consensus building, and planning for action.
- Ground rules for decision making are agreed on, known, followed, and regularly reassessed.
- Conflict resolution strategies have been agreed on, are taught, and are practiced.

Student discipline

- Expectations for student behavior are reasonable, positive, public, known, and enforced with consistency.
- Classroom discipline is dealt with primarily by the classroom teacher; there are very few referrals to the office for disrespect.
- The school "disciplinarian" does not spend the majority of his or her time disciplining students; rather he or she spends considerable time working positively with teachers, students, parents, and the community.
- Student discipline is done privately, in a problem-solving mode. (At Central Park East Secondary School, the habits of mind are used in student discipline situations to focus students on solving the underlying problem.)

Teacher as adviser

- No secondary school teacher is responsible for more than 90 students.
- A strong student advisory system is in place. Advisories will not work in schools where teachers are responsible for large numbers of students.
- Teachers maintain regular contact with parents regarding student progress, including positive feedback.

- Teachers, parents, and students collaborate to develop an individual learning plan for each student.

Teacher as collaborator

- Teachers can be seen working in a collegial school culture—adults talk with one another, observe one another, help one another, laugh together, and celebrate together.
- Conversations in the faculty room are lively, with teachers talking positively about students, student work, their own work, and the work of colleagues.
- Faculty and staff are not seen brooding in the faculty room or in the parking lot or segregated by sex, race, department, or age.
- Time and resources are provided for teachers to collaborate.

High Expectations and Purposeful Change

What does a school look like whose culture is centered on high expectations and purposeful support?

- Reasonable, positive, public, known, and consistently enforced policies and procedures are in place.
- The campus is well maintained, with little litter and graffiti.
- A broad range of student work is on display throughout the school.
- Every student can name at least two adults who know him or her well and his or her work well.
- The parent's role in supporting student learning is valued and supported through parent workshops, a parent library, and the availability of social services support.
- Members of the community are seen supporting student learning; space and training are provided for this purpose.
- Teachers, parents, and students talk openly about the commitment of the principal and district to all students learning to use their minds and hearts well.
- Staff articulate a common mission that all agree transcends personal differences.

What are curriculum, instruction, and assessment like in a school that is designed to foster high expectations and purposeful support for all students?

Curriculum

- Students are actively engaged in interdisciplinary, thematic, project-based work.
- Projects have significance to students and are based on important questions raised by students, teachers, and community members.
- Curriculum respects and acknowledges the ethnography and community of the students, using this as a departure point for curriculum that explores diversity of culture and opinion within and without the community.
- Teachers individualize and modify instruction that addresses learning styles and the special needs of students.
- Students comment (or proudly complain) that the work is challenging and takes time.

Instruction

- Classes are heterogeneously grouped for most of the day, with regrouping as appropriate.
- Students usually are working in small groups or independently.
- There is a well-defined safety net in place to accelerate students who are falling behind in their academic progress.
- Common instructional strategies are being used in most classrooms within and across grade levels.
- When teachers ask questions, students are required to use higher-order thinking skills to answer, and all students have equal access to respond.
- When students ask questions, teachers usually reply with a question that requires thought by the student, rather than with the answer.

Assessment

- Student learning is assessed in a variety of ways, including the use of well-publicized rubrics, public exhibitions, and self-reflection by students.
- Individual teachers use assessment strategies on a daily basis to diagnose the learning of individual students and to adjust instruction based on this assessment.
- Teachers review student work and other assessment data together to guide school and classroom practice.
- When asked, students talk articulately about their best work.

How do teacher and administrator roles change in such a school?

- The principal knows students and their work well and is often seen engaged in conversations with teachers about individual students and their learning.
- The principal knows students and their work well and is often seen engaged in conversations with students about their learning.
- Teachers and school and district administrators have agreed-on best practices in a limited number of areas of focus (literacy, habits of mind), and time, resources, and professional development are supporting implementation—including expert and peer coaching and collaborative action research.
- Time is provided for teachers to discuss the needs and successes of individual students.
- Time is provided for teachers to discuss classroom practice.
- Teachers talk openly about how supportive the principal and district are regarding supporting ideas and helping to provide resources.

Meaningful Participation

What does a school look like whose culture is centered on meaningful participation by all students?

- Students are working in the library, computer lab, laboratories, and hallways, individually and collaboratively with peers.

- Students are engaged in *required helpfulness:*
  - Older students are seen working with younger students.
  - Students are engaged with peers as peer helpers, conflict resolvers, and tutors.
  - Students spend time each week in service learning projects on and off campus.
- Class meetings and schoolwide forums are held regularly to gather student input regarding meaningful school issues. These meetings are often facilitated by students.
- An effort is being made to include all student groups in the daily life of the school; students are not seen on the fringes of the school campus, alienated and voicing displeasure with the school, staff, and peers.
- A large percentage of the students participate in and lead a wide range of school activities.
- Signs on campus encourage students to join activities and do not indicate hurdles to complete; the words "students must" do not appear on school postings.
- Time is provided at least weekly for teachers to work together on curriculum, instruction, and assessment.
- Most students, faculty, and staff are known and welcomed by name, and many parents and community members are known and welcomed by name.
- Drug, alcohol, smoking, and fighting infractions are statistically small and show an annual decrease.

What are curriculum, instruction, and assessment like in a school that is designed to foster meaningful participation by all students?

Curriculum

- Curriculum is project based, set around complex issues, some of which relate to school and community issues.
- Students have choices in the specifics of what they investigate, how they do the investigation, and how they demonstrate what they have learned.
- Service learning is a part of every student's academic program.

Instruction

- Teachers ask students questions that require students to do critical, reflective thinking, such as the questions associated with Anzar and CPESS's habits of mind.
- Teachers spend much of their time coaching students, and students spend much of their time working individually and in small groups.
- Students are usually not sitting in desks in rows.
- Students are not seen sitting unengaged in the back of classrooms.
- School resources are readily available; computers and resource materials are easy for students to access.

Assessment

- Students exhibit and reflect on what they have learned.
- Standards for quality work are well-known, and often designed with student input.
- Teachers use student work to guide classroom and school practices.

How do teacher and administrator roles change in such a school?

- Principals, teachers, students, parents, community members, and classified staff are engaged in schoolwide decision making around issues of substance, including establishing school priorities, budgeting to support those priorities, and hiring personnel.
- Norms for decision making, consensus building, and conflict resolution are mutually agreed on, followed, and regularly reassessed.
- Meetings focus on meaningful input and decision making rather than information giving; agendas are posted with opportunities for agenda input; relevant information is provided ahead of meetings; participants are at meetings on time; meetings start on time and end on time.

- Divergent thinking is encouraged and heard in formal meetings and in informal conversations.
- Put-downs, side conversations, and comments that indicate exclusion are not heard in or out of meetings.
- Mistakes are celebrated as learning experiences, and responsibility for mistakes is shared without blame.
- Teachers work collegially, sharing curriculum and instructional strategies, talking about students and student work, coaching each other to be more effective. Time and resources are provided to support this.
- Teachers talk freely about feeling valued by administrators, parents, and students as participants in the whole school community.
- Administrators, faculty, classified staff, students, and parents seem to enjoy being together; across roles, people seek each other out, talk together, laugh together.
- Faculty and staff are not seen brooding in the faculty room or in the parking lot.
- Students are given classroom and schoolwide responsibilities of increasing importance with age.

Resource B

Assessing School Resiliency Building

Evaluate the following elements of school resiliency building using a scale of 1 to 4, with 1 indicating "We have this together," 2 indicating "We've done a lot in this area, but could do more," 3 indicating "We are getting started," and 4 indicating "Nothing has been done."

Prosocial Bonding

____ Students have a positive bond with at least one caring adult in the school.

____ Students are engaged in lots of interest-based before, after, and during school activities.

____ Staff engage in meaningful interactions with one another.

____ Staff have been involved in creating meaningful vision and mission statements.

____ Families are positively bonded to the school.

SOURCE: Henderson and Milstein (1996).

____ The physical environment of the school is warm, positive, and inviting.

____ **Total Score**

Clear, Consistent Boundaries

____ Students are clear about the behaviors expected of them and experience consistency in boundary enforcement.

____ Students use an intervention process (core or care team) that helps them when they are having problems.

____ Staff are clear about what is expected of them and experience consistency of expectations.

____ Staff model the behavioral expectations developed for students and adults.

____ The school fosters an ongoing discussion of norms, rules, goals, and expectations for staff and students.

____ The school provides training necessary for members of the school community to set and live by behavioral expectations.

____ **Total Score**

Teaching Life Skills

____ Students use refusal skills, assertiveness, healthy conflict resolution, good decision making and problem solving, and healthy stress-management skills most of the time.

____ Students are engaged in cooperative learning that focuses on both social skills and academic outcomes.

____ Staff work cooperatively together and emphasize the importance of cooperation.

____ Staff have the interpersonal skills necessary to engage in effective organizational functioning and the professional skills necessary for effective teaching.

____ The school provides the skill development needed by all members of the school community.

____ The school promotes a philosophy of lifelong learning.

____ **Total Score**

Caring and Support

____ Students feel cared for and supported in the school.
____ Students experience many types of incentives, recognition, and rewards.
____ Staff feel cared for and appreciated in the school.
____ Staff experience many types of incentives, recognition, and rewards.
____ The school has a climate of kindness and encouragement.
____ Resources needed by students and staff are secured and distributed fairly in the school.
____ **Total Score**

High Expectations

____ Students believe that they can succeed.
____ Students experience little or no labeling (formally or informally) or tracking.
____ Staff believe members can succeed.
____ Staff are rewarded for risk taking and excellence (e.g., merit pay).
____ The school provides growth plans for staff and students with clear outcomes, regular reviews, and supportive feedback.
____ An attitude of "can do" permeates the school.
____ **Total Score**

Opportunities for Meaningful Participation

____ Students are involved in programs that emphasize service to other students, the school, and the community.
____ Students are involved in school decision making, including governance and policy.
____ Staff are involved in school decision making, including governance and policy.
____ Staff are engaged in both job-specific and organization-wide responsibilities.

___ Everyone in the school community (students, parents, staff) is viewed as a resource rather than as a problem, object, or client.

___ The school climate emphasizes "doing what really matters" and risk taking.

___ **Total Score**

___ Overall Assessment Score (total of each of the six sections)
Student   ___   (total of the first two scores in each section)
Staff   ___   (total of the second two scores in each section)
School   ___   (total of the last two scores in each section)

Range of scores: overall, 36-144; each section, 6-24; students, staff, and the school, 12-48. Lower scores indicate positive resilience building; higher scores indicate a need for improvement.

Resource C

Moving From Risk to Resiliency
in Our Schools

Creating Opportunities to Learn	
From	To
Relationships Between and Among Teachers, Students, Parents	
Hierarchical, blaming, controlling	Characterized by caring, positive expectations and participation
Teacher Behavior and Attitudes	
Conveys message: This work is required; you may not be able to do it; you're on your own. Looks for deficiencies	Conveys message: This work is important; I know you can do it; I won't give up on you. Looks for strengths
Physical Environment	
Peeling paint; boarded windows; dirty; things don't work; graffiti	Painted; clean; works; kids' work on display

Curriculum and Instruction	
Fragmented, nonexperiential; Eurocentric focus; limited access to broad variety of courses and activities; teaches to narrow range of learning styles; status quo	Integrated, experience-based/service learning; college core/enrichment available to all students; reflects cultures of all students; access to broad variety of courses and activities; teaches to broad range learning styles; critical inquiry
Grouping	
Homogenous; tracking; individual competition; pull-out programs	Heterogeneous; untracked; cooperative groups; inclusive all students; "families"
Evaluation	
Assess only limited range of intelligences; standardized; focus on "right" answers	Assess multiple intelligences; holistic; authentic, portfolio; fosters self-reflection
Motivation	
Competitive; extrinsic rewards; no involvement in meaningful decision making	Collaborating; intrinsic rewards; active engagement—connected to learner's interest, strengths, and real world
Responsibility	
Authority-determined rules; "sage on state"/dictator; no involvement in meaningful decision making	Democratic, consensual; "guide on side"/facilitator; active participation in decision-making peer helping, community service

Resource D. Cupertino Union School District, Junior High Assessment. Standard 1: Student/School Connectedness

Category 1A. Caring and Support

Level 1 *Initial Stage*	Level 2 *Emerging*	Level 3 *Becoming*	Level 4 *Maturing*	Level 5 *Accomplished/Refining*
Little thought has been given to examining the norms, practices, and policies of the school to ensure a safe and caring community.	The staff see creating a safe and caring community as a goal. Most changes in norms, practices, and policies occur as reactions to specific problems.	The school has systematically studied the effect of its norms, practices, and policies on students and adults and is implementing changes to create a safe and caring community for all.	Most norms, practices, and policies of the school result in students and adults experiencing the school as a safe and caring community.	The school community regularly examines and refines the norms, practices, and policies of the school, ensuring a safe and caring community for all students and adults.
The school culture equates harshness with high standards. Adults who model caring and support tend to be viewed as "pushovers."	The staff respect adults who model caring and support in their interactions with students, families, and each other.	Although most adults have agreed to model caring and support in their interactions, many revert to previous practices under stress.	With peer support, most adults have learned to model caring and support in their interactions with students, families, and each other.	All adults model caring and support in their interactions with students, families, and each other.

162

Teachers and counselors see too many students to know them well. Student advising focuses on scheduling.	Fragmented changes have been implemented to form deeper connections between staff and students, with varying success.	A more systematic approach to make sure that every student is well-known by a significant adult on the campus is being implemented.	Most students and families are well-known by one or more significant adults on campus, who act as their advocates.	All students and their families feel connected to and are well known by one or more significant adults on campus, who act as their advocates.
Most teachers focus on academics, while other personnel attend to other student needs.* Students who require additional services are viewed as a burden.	Many staff members see the importance of developing all* aspects of each student. Some work individually to meet these needs.	There is a school-wide focus on developing all* aspects of each student that is also reflected in the school plan. Some support systems are in place.	There is a school-wide focus on developing all* aspects of each student that is also reflected in the school plan. Support systems are in place.	There is clear evidence that a coherent, school-wide focus on developing all* aspects of each student is resulting in improved student access.

*Academic, intellectual, social, emotional, cultural, and linguistic

Category 1B. Meaningful Student Participation

Level 1 *Initial Stage*	Level 2 *Emerging*	Level 3 *Becoming*	Level 4 *Maturing*	Level 5 *Accomplished/Refining*
Adults rarely seek input for decisions from students. When sought, input comes from a small number of student leaders.	Adults regularly seek input for decisions from student leadership groups, but only occasionally from other students.	Adults regularly seek input for decisions from students, both at the classroom and at the schoolwide level. Final decisions sometimes reflect this input.	Input is regularly sought from students, both at the classroom and at the schoolwide level. Students participate in the consensus process for many decisions.	Students have an authentic voice in decision making, both at the classroom and at the schoolwide level.
Almost all school activities are designed and controlled by adults. Students have little opportunity to develop skills in making choices, self-assessing, or developing responsibility.	Some extracurricular and/or classroom activities provide opportunities for students to develop skills in making choices, self-assessing, and developing responsibility.	There is a schoolwide effort to make changes in classroom and extracurricular activities to provide opportunities for students to develop skills in making choices, self-assessing, or developing responsibility.	In most classrooms and extracurricular activities, students are encouraged to make choices, be self-assessing, and take personal responsibility.	Throughout the school, activities are designed to ensure student choice, self-assessment, and personal responsibility.

Many students feel unwanted or unaccepted in school-sponsored activities due to real or perceived barriers such as competition and popularity. School-sponsored activities are separate from the instructional program.	An effort is being made by many staff to include more students in school activities by breaking down real or perceived barriers.	The school community has carefully assessed what real or perceived barriers exist to participation in school activities and is beginning to implement a systematic plan to improve access.	Many students take advantage of the multiple opportunities to be involved in activities that connect to their individual interests and abilities and to the academic program. Involvement in school activities reflects the diversity of the school.	Most students take advantage of the multiple opportunities to be involved in activities that connect to their individual interests and abilities and to the instructional program. Involvement in school-sponsored activities reflects the diversity of the school.

Category 1C. Community-Building Efforts

Level 1 Initial Stage	Level 2 Emerging	Level 3 Becoming	Level 4 Maturing	Level 5 Accomplished/Refining
There is no schoolwide effort to teach effective conflict resolution, problem-solving, and communication skills.	The need to teach effective conflict resolution, problem-solving, and communication skills has been identified. Some implementation of programs designed to teach these skills may be evident, but not in all classrooms.	The school has begun to implement a school-wide plan to train all members of the school community in conflict resolution, problem solving, and communication.	All students and adults have been trained in effective conflict resolution, problem-solving, and communication skills. The practice of these skills is evident and is reinforced through peer support.	All students and adults practice effective conflict resolution, problem-solving, and communication skills.
Most students are afraid of judgment by teachers and peers if they express their feelings and ideas.	Although staff believe that students should feel free to express their feelings and ideas, most students still fear judgment by teachers and peers.	Students are comfortable expressing their feelings and ideas without fear of judgment much of the time.	Students are comfortable expressing their feelings and ideas without fear of judgment most of the time.	Students are comfortable expressing their feelings and ideas without fear of judgment and are encouraged to do so.

Students in different grades have little opportunity to interact with each other. Younger students may be intimidated by older students.	Interaction across grades occurs in school activities and a few electives.	Systems are being developed to create close bonds and support between students of different grades.	Systems exist to create close bonds and support between students of different grades.	Systems exist that result in close bonds and support between students of different grades. The whole school community assesses and refines these structures.
Community service, if performed at all, is a function of extra-curricular clubs that draw students who are already actively involved in the school.	Community service is seen as valuable, but conflicting with academic time. A few teachers occasionally include a community service project in their programs.	Conceptually, service learning is embraced by the school. Community service projects may be required in a few classes, or as an addition to the program.	A coherent community service learning component has been developed as part of the instructional program. Students have input into the program.	Students feel connected to school through community service learning experiences that are an integral part of the instructional program. Students have choices and input in community service learning projects.

167

Category 1D. Partnerships

Level 1 Initial Stage	Level 2 Emerging	Level 3 Becoming	Level 4 Maturing	Level 5 Accomplished/Refining
A small number of active parents influences the school policies on behalf of students. Many staff members view parents as interfering in the school.	The school community sees the value of increased parent involvement. Attempts to increase involvement are unfocused and yield mixed results.	By assessing real and perceived barriers, the school community has determined how to broaden parent involvement in the life of the school and is implementing a plan for improvement.	A growing cross-section of the parent community feels connected to the school and actively participates in planning, implementing, assessing, and refining the school's improvement efforts.	A broad cross-section of the parent community feels connected to the school and actively participates in planning, implementing, assessing, and refining the school's improvement efforts.
Parents are contacted only when their student has a serious school-related problem. As a result, students fear home-school communication.	Parents are contacted when their students has a problem. Parents are also invited to request conferences, but few actually do. Most students fear home-school communication.	Community needs have been studied to determine what systems would best result in frequent staff-student-parent interactive communication; implementation has begun. Student involvement results in decreased fear of home-school communication.	Some systems are in place that result in regular staff-student-parent interactive communication to support each student's success. Initial student and parent reactions to these experiences are positive.	Systems are in place that result in regular staff-student-parent interactive communication to support each student's success. Students experience home-school communication as a way of sharing their goals and progress with parents.

Allocating district and school resources to improve student connectedness is a low priority.	The district and school agree that resources should be allocated to support student connectedness. In the absence of an overall plan, efforts may be fragmented.	Both the district and the school better understand how to allocate combined resources to support student-school connectedness.	The district-school partnership allows for resources to be allocated to support student-school connectedness.	The district-school partnership ensures that resources are allocated and used well to support student-school connectedness.
Referrals for family services are not viewed as a school responsibility. Parents are expected to seek the services they need through outside agencies.	A counselor or other staff member provides referrals to family services in the community on request or when a need is identified.	The school is actively seeking partnerships with community agencies to support the student/family needs based on a careful assessment.	Partnerships have been formed with several community agencies to support the needs of individual students and families explicitly.	School/community agency partnerships explicitly support the needs of students and families and services are continuously assessed and improved by the partners.
Use of outside agencies is inconsistent and infrequent. Follow-up on referrals seldom occurs.	Outside agencies that provide services determine whether their services are respectful, accessible, and appropriate.	Discussions are under way to ensure that services from outside agencies are respectful, accessible, and appropriate.	Many services from outside agencies to students and their families are respectful, accessible, and appropriate.	Most services from outside agencies to students and their families are respectful and have been organized to ensure easy access and continuity.

Resource E
Questions for Reflection

Chapter 1

Think back on your own schooling. Who cared deeply about you? Who held high expectations for you and supported you to meet these expectations? Who valued your participation?

Think back on your own childhood. Who cared deeply about you? Who held high expectations for you and supported you to meet these expectations? Who valued your participation?

Think about times when the protective factors were missing from your life? How did this feel? What did you do to cope? What did you learn about yourself and others from these experiences?

Talk with someone who overcame great adversity. To what or whom does this person attribute his or her success? What did this person do to cope? What did he or she learn about himself or herself and others from these experiences?

Think about three students whom you know well and who are different from each other. What does their school do to foster resiliency for each of these students? Specifically, what do people at the school do to help each of them feel cared for, know that expectations are high and support is strong, and know that their participation in the life of the school and classroom is valued? What do each of these students need to experience a more resilient learning community at the school? Use these students as a lens as you continue reading this book and as you look at your school.

Chapter 2

Do you believe that all students are capable of doing intellectually challenging work?

Think about the three students you reflected on in Chapter 1. Do you believe that each is capable of intellectually challenging work? What evidence do you have? What do you do to challenge each of these students, and how do you support their work?

Chapter 3

Examine your own resiliency. When and how have you overcome adversity? Who and what helped you? What strengths did you gain?

What kind of support do you expect from people you work with? How well do you know the work of people you work with? How well do they know your work?

What do you do to build professional relationships? Do you enjoy "talking shop"? Does such talk help make you more effective? Who do you work with who challenges you to think about what you do?

Do you feel respected by the people you work for and with? How do they show you respect or lack of respect? Do you respect these people? How do you show them respect or lack of respect?

Do you feel listened to at work? Who values your opinion? How do they show you? Do you value what others have to say? How do you let them know?

What and who brings you joy at work? What do you do to build these people and these activities into your daily work life?

If you use the following questions to assess your school, particularly if you insist on specific evidence, you will learn a lot about the belief system that guides the daily practices of the school.

- How successful is your school in meeting the needs of your students?
- Which students are you doing an excellent job for? Which students could you serve better?
- What specific evidence do you have to support your answers to these two questions?
- What is blocking your school from being more successful?
- What are the underlying beliefs of your school culture that support these blocks?
- What needs to change for your school to be more successful?
- What specific evidence do you have to support your answers to these last three questions?

- What percentage of the students at your school does the principal know by name?
- What percentage of the students do most teachers know by name?
- What percentage of the teachers and classified staff do all teachers and classified staff know by name?

Look at how time is used at your school.

- How engaging are staff meetings at your school? Leadership team meetings? Home and school club meetings? Professional development activities?
- How much time do teachers spend working with individual students or students in small groups, really getting to know students and their work well?
- How much time do teachers spend working with other teachers in small groups, really getting to know teachers and their work well?

Chapter 4

Shadow a student for a school day. Sit in classes, eat meals with the student, check out the restrooms, observe the peer relationships as a student does. What is it like to be a student at this school?

Chapter 5

Spend an hour talking with each of the three students you identified in Chapter 1. Does each one of these students feel known within the school? Does each one feel that his or her work is known? Does each one feel that he or she is supported to meet high expectations?

Think about your three students. What support is in place within the school to help assure that they acquire strong habits of mind?

Chapter 6

Think about your high school years. What are your most powerful and valuable memories? It doesn't matter whether these are positive or negative. You should have several examples in mind. Eliminate any that involve athletics, the fine and performing arts, school leadership activities, and school social life. Focus only on memories from academic classes. Next, and harder to do, eliminate the memory if it is primarily associated with the charisma of the teacher. Write down whatever you still have in mind.

Talk with your three students again. How engaged are they in what happens in their classes and in the life of the school? What influence do they feel they have on the school?

Talk with three teachers and three classified staff members. How engaged do they feel they are in what happens in the life of the school? Talk with the principal. How engaged is the principal in what happens in classrooms and in the district? What influence do these teachers, classified staff, and principal feel they have on the school?

Chapter 7

Think of an important change that happened in your life. What caused it? How did you respond to it? What did you learn about yourself?

Think about how you handled the death of someone close to you. How did you react? What did you learn about yourself? Many people react to change in the workplace in ways similar to dealing with a death.

Think about reactions from people you know and from yourself to change. Is there blaming? At what stage? What happens to stop the blaming? Or, what should have happened to prevent blaming?

References

Agee, J., & Evans, W. (1960). *Let us now praise famous men.* Cambridge: Riverside.

Barnett, D., McKowen, C., & Bloom, G. (1998). A school without a principal. *Educational Leadership, 55*(7), 48-49.

Barth, R. (1991). *Improving schools from within: Teachers, parents, and principals can make a difference.* San Francisco: Jossey-Bass.

Benard, B. (1991). *Fostering resiliency in kids: Protective factors in the family, school, and community.* Portland, OR: Western Center for Drug-Free Schools and Communities.

Benard, B. (1993). Fostering resiliency in kids. *Educational Leadership, 51*(3), 44-48.

Benard, B. (1995). Fostering resilience in children. *ERIC Digest.* Urbana, IL: ERIC.

Bridges, W. (1991). *Managing transitions: Making the most of change.* Reading, MA: Addison-Wesley.

Burns, T., & Lofquist, B. (1996). *The next step: Integrating resiliency and community development in the school.* Tucson: Development Publications.

Butler, K. (1997, March/April). The anatomy of resilience. *Networker,* pp. 22-31.

Chaleff, I. (1995). *The courageous follower: Standing up to and for our leaders.* San Francisco: Berrett-Koehler.

Cummins, J. (1996). *Negotiating identities: Education for empowerment in a diverse society.* Ontario: California Association for Bilingual Education.

Cushman, K. (1995). Making the good school better: The essential question of rigor. *Horace, 11*(4), 1-8.

Darling-Hammond, L., Ancess, J., & Falk, B. (1995). *Authentic assessment in action: Studies of schools and students at work.* New York: Teachers College Press.

Evans, R. (1996). *The human side of school change.* San Francisco: Jossey-Bass.

Felner, R. D., Jackson, A., Kasak, D., Mulhall, P., Brand, S., & Flowers, N. (in press). The impact of school reform for the middle years: A longitudinal study of a network engaged in turning points-based comprehensive school transformation. In R. Takanishi & D. Hamburg (Eds.), *Preparing young adolescents for the 21st century: Challenges for Europe and the United States.* New York: Cambridge University Press.

Henderson, N., & Milstein, M. M. (1996). *Resiliency in schools: Making it happen for students and educators.* Thousand Oaks, CA: Corwin.

Kitashima, M. (1997). The faces of resiliency: Lessons from my life: No more "children at risk" . . . all children are "at promise." *Resiliency in Action, 2*(3), 30-36.

Klonsky, M. (1996). *Small schools: The numbers tell a story.* Chicago: University of Illinois at Chicago.

Krovetz, M. L., & Cohick, D. (1993). Professional collegiality can lead to school change. *Kappan, 75,* 331-333.

Kyle, R. (1993). *Transforming our schools: Lessons from the Jefferson County public schools/Gheens Professional Development Academy (1983-1991).* Louisville, KY: Gheens Foundation.

Lee, V. E., & Smith, J. B. (1994). *Effects of high school restructuring and size on gains in achievement and engagement for early secondary school students.* Madison, WI: Center on Organization and Restructuring of Schools.

Lezin, N. (1997, March). *Keynote address.* Presented at the first annual awards banquet for Schools Plus, Public Schools Foundation for Santa Cruz Country, Santa Cruz, CA.

Lieberman, A. (Ed.). (1995). *The work of restructuring schools: Building from the ground up.* New York: Teachers College Press.

McDonald, J. (1996). *Redesigning schools: Lessons for the 21st century.* San Francisco: Jossey-Bass.

Meier, D. (1995). *The power of their ideas.* Boston: Beacon.

Newmann, F. M., & Wehlage, G. G. (1995). *Successful school restructuring: A report to the public and educators by the Center on Organization and Restructuring of Schools.* Madison, WI: Center on Organization and Restructuring Schools.

Nieto, S. (1996). *Affirming diversity: The sociopolitical context of multicultural education.* New York: Longman.

Noddings, N. (1995). A morally defensible mission for schools in the 21st century. *Kappan, 76*(5), 365-368.

Poplin, M., & Weeres, J. (1994). *Voices from the inside: A report on schooling from inside the classroom.* Claremont, CA: Institute for Education in Transformation.

Powell, A. G., Farrar, E., & Cohen, D. K. (1985). *The shopping mall high school: Winners and losers in the educational marketplace.* Boston: Houghton Mifflin.

Rutter, M. (1979). *Fifteen thousand hours: Secondary schools and their effects on children.* Cambridge, MA: Harvard University Press.

Sarason, S. (1990). *The predictable failure of educational reform.* San Francisco: Jossey-Bass.

Shapiro, J. P., Friedman, D., Meyer, M., & Loftus, M. (1996, November 11). Invincible kids. *U.S. News and World Report,* pp. 62-71.

Sizer, T. R. (1985). *Horace's compromise.* Boston: Houghton Mifflin.

Sizer, T. R. (1992). *Horace's school.* Boston: Houghton Mifflin.

Sizer, T. R. (1996). *Horace's hope.* Boston: Houghton Mifflin.

Speck, M., & Krovetz, M. L. (1995). Student resiliency: Building caring learning communities. *Multicultures, 1,* 113-123.

Swanson, M. C. (1993). The AVID story: Advancement via individual determination. *Thrust for Educational Leadership, 22*(6), 8-12.

University-School Support for Educational Reform. (1997). *Essential questions and practices in professional development.* San Francisco: Author.

Wang, M. C., Haertel, G. D., & Walberg, H. J. (1995) *Educational resilience: An emergent construct.* Philadelphia: National Center on Education in the Inner Cities.

Weissbourd, R. (1996). *The vulnerable child: What really hurts America's children and what we can do about it.* Reading, MA: Addison-Wesley.

Werner, E. (1996). How children become resilient: Observations and cautions. *Resiliency in Action, 1*(1), 18-28.

Werner, E., & Smith, R. S. (1992). *Overcoming the odds: High risk children from birth to adulthood.* Ithaca, NY: Cornell University Press.

Wolfson, J., & Leyba, J. (1997, February 23). The resolution in turning inspiration into innovation in the Silicon Valley: Steve Wozniak. *San Jose Mercury News,* pp. 1A, 20A-21A.

Index

Academic intervention, 81-82

Action plan, 114-115

Affiliation, social, 4-5

Anzar High School, xi, xv, 2
  givens, school culture, 14, 15
    (figure)
  graduation by exhibition, 14-18
  habits of mind, 14, 16 (figure), 24
  history of, 12-13
  planning time, 19
  snapshot, 11-12, 19-21
  teachers as leaders, 18-19

Assessment, 63, 68, 85, 98, 152, 154

Association for Supervision and
  Curriculum Development
  (ASCD) National Restructuring
  Collaborative, xvii

At-risk population, 6-10, 138

Bay Area School Reform Collaborative (BASRC), 11, 114

Benard, Bonnie, xi, xiii, 22, 138

Bridges, William, xii, 108, 116

Campbell Union Elementary
  School District, xi

Caring:
  curriculum, instruction, and as-
    sessment, 61-63, 148
  resiliency building, 158
  risk to resiliency, movement
    from, 162-163
  school culture of, 60-61, 141,
    146-147, 173
  teacher/administrator role
    change, 63-64, 149-150

Case studies:
  Anzar High School, 2, 11-21
  Cesar Chavez School, 47-56
  Homestead High School, 99-105
  Mission Hill Junior High
    School, 122-136
  Moss Landing Middle School,
    65-72
  Rosemary School, 22, 26-34
  Stipe School, 86-92

Central Park East Secondary
  School, 76

Cesar Chavez School, xi, xv
    collegiality, 51-52
    history of, 49-50
    job satisfaction, 54-55
    obstacles to learning, 55
    professional development, 52
    respect, 53
    snapshot, 47-49, 50-51
    student outcomes, 55-56
    voice, 53-54
Change, xii, 46, 78, 106-107
    action plan development, 114-115
    conversations, essential, 109-
        112, 138-139
    effectiveness evaluation, 115-
        116, 140-141
    inclusion and, 139
    leadership, 108-109, 118-119
    management of, 119-120, 120
        (figure)
    personalizing schools, 83
    problem identification, 117-118
    reflective questions, 174-175
    resistance to, 120-121, 139-140
    school culture and, 108
    school resiliency, assessment of,
        112-114, 113 (figure), 114
        (figure)
    self-assessment, 109, 110 (figure),
        174-175
    transition, 107-108, 116-117
    See also Restructuring; School
        practices
Children:
    resiliency attributes, 7, 9, 64-65
    supporting resiliency in, 10-11
Coalition of Essential Schools, 2, 12
Community. See Resilient commu-
    nity; School community, resilient
Curriculum, 62, 68, 84, 97, 151, 153

Evans, Robert, 108
Exhibition for graduation:
    components of, 15-17
    habits of mind and, 14, 16 (figure)
    teacher commitment to, 17-18
Expectations, high, 73-74

belief system, practice of, 78-80,
    138, 150
curriculum, instruction, and
    assessment, 151-152
engagement, low level of, 74-75
habits of mind, 76-77
literacy, 75, 141
reflective questions, 173-174
resiliency building, 158
teacher/administrator role
    changes, 152
tracking, 77-78
See also Support, purposeful

Gangs, 3-4

Habits of mind, 14, 16 (figure), 24,
    73, 76-77
Homestead High School, xii, xv
    distinguishing factors of, 102-103
    history of, 100-101
    problem-solving snapshot, 99-100
    redesign framework, 102
    revisioning snapshot, 101-102
    student outcomes, 104-105

Inclusion, 139
Instruction, 62-63, 68, 84, 97-98,
    151, 154

Learning community, resilient. See
    School community, resilient
Learning opportunities, creation
    of, 160-161

Meier, Debbie, 62
Mentoring programs, 81
    academic intervention and, 81-82
    incentives and 82-83
Mind/heart engagement, 24
Mission Hill Junior High School,
    xii, xv
    activities, restructuring, 123-124
    anticipation vs. experience, 127-
        128
    envisioning change, 124-126
    history of, 134-135

restructuring, focus of, 122-123
student outcomes, 135-136
year four and five of restructuring, 132
year one of restructuring, 128-130
year six—reassessment, 132-134
year three—sky's the limit, 131-132
year two of restructuring, 130-131
Moss Landing Middle School
(MLMS), xi, xv
caring, 65-66
focus, clarity of, 67, 68-69 (figure)
history of, 66-67
practices supporting focus, 67-71
student outcomes, 71-72

Obstacles to resiliency, 40-41
school practices, 41-42
school size, 42-43
simple fixes, 44-45
time constraints, 43-44
Outcomes. *See* Student outcomes

Participation, 93-94
curriculum, instruction, and assessment, 97-98, 153-154
elements of, 96-97, 152-153
inclusive, 95-96
protective factor, 94-95
reflective questions, 174
resiliency-building, 158-159
risk to resiliency, movement from, 164-165
teacher/administrator role change, 98-99, 154-155
Peer relationships, 4-5
Peer support, 82
Practices. *See* School practices
Problem focus model, 6
Protective factors, 2, 10, 35-36
Public schools, 47

Research, 7, 8-9 (figure)
Resiliency:
abuse of term, xiv
adult practitioners and, 141-142

at-risk populations and, 6-10, 138
defined, 2
district initiatives and, 138
effectiveness evaluation, 140-141
habits of mind, 14, 16 (figure), 24, 73, 137
institutional support of, x
protective factors of, 2, 10, 35-36
reflective questions on, 170-171
schools and, 45-47
See also Obstacles to resiliency;
Risk to resiliency; School community, resilient
Resiliency building:
boundaries, clear and consistent, 157
caring and support, 158
expectations, high, 158
life skills, teaching of, 157
participation, meaningful, 158-159
prosocial bonding, 156-157
Resiliency prerequisite model, 23-26, 24 (figure)
Resiliency theory (RT), ix-x, 7
attributes of resilient children, 7, 9
research foundation of, 8-9
Resilient communities:
defined, 2, 10, 121
gangs as, 3-4
obstacles to, 40-45
schools as, 3, 6, 11
See also School community, resilient
Restructuring, xii, 122-123, 138-139
Risk to resiliency, movement from:
caring and support, 162-163
community-building, 166-167
learning opportunities, creation of, 160-161
participation, meaningful, 164-165
partnerships in, 168-169
Rosemary School, xi, xv, 22
belief system, 30

change, managing and leading, 32
collegiality, 30-31
history of, 29
professionalism, 31-32
resiliency in, 32-33
snapshot, 26-29
student outcomes, 33-34

School choice, 47
School community, resilient, 3, 6
collegiality, 36-37, 137
effectiveness assessment, 112-114, 113 (figure), 114 (figure)
habits of mind, 14, 16 (figure), 24, 73, 137
job satisfaction, 39-40
obstacles to resiliency, 40-45
personalization in, 83
professionalism, 37-38
protective factors, 35-36
reflective questions, 171
resiliency prerequisite model, 23-26, 24 (figure)
respect, atmosphere of, 38-39
voice, 39
See also Caring; Change
School practices:
mind/heart engagement, 25
redesigning, x, xii
resiliency in, 3
shame/devaluation, 5-6
student outcomes, effect on, xiii
See also Change; Restructuring; School community, resilient
Shame/devaluation, 5-6
Smith, Ruth, xi, 7, 8-9 (figure), 138
Social affiliation, 4-5
Speck, Marsha, 23

Stipe School, xii, xv
distinguishing factors, 87-90
history of, 87
snapshot, 86-87
student outcomes, 91-92
Student outcomes:
measures of, xiii
student/teacher relationships and, 57-58, 138
Support, purposeful, 73-74, 81-83 (figure)
characteristics of, 80, 84, 150
curriculum, instruction, and assessment and, 84-85
risk to resiliency, movement from, 162-163
teacher/administrator role changes, 85
Systemic change. See Change; Restructuring; School practices

Teachers:
collegiality, 25-26, 36-37
professionalism, 26, 37-38
resiliency and, 95-96, 141-142, 171-173
resisting change, 120-121
student relationships with, 57-58
See also School community, resilient
Teaching. See Instruction
Tracking, 77-78
Transition, 107-108, 116-117

Vargo, Merrill, 11

Werner, Emmy, x, xi, xiv, 7, 8-9 (figure), 75, 138